I0840989

Reloading
7.62x51mm
Military Brass

Target Loads

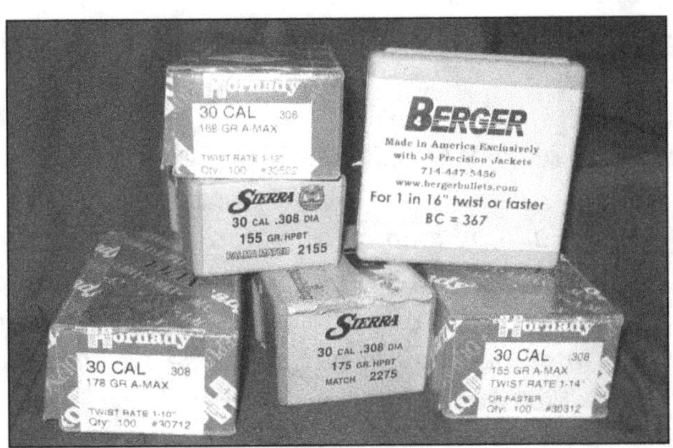

**All data was developed using
a heavy barreled Tikka T3 bolt action rifle.**

Stephen Redgwell
303british.com
2009

Copyright © 2009 by Stephen Redgwell

No part of this book may be reproduced or transmitted in any form or by any means, electronic or mechanical, including photocopying and recording, or by any information storage or retrieval system without written permission from the author, except for brief passages quoted in a review.

Redgwell, Stephen, 1956 -
Reloading 7.62x51mm military brass

Distributed by:
303british.com

To Order: Write or visit http://www.303british.com

WARNING: *The author cannot be responsible for accidental or incidental injury or damage that result from user errors or improper use. I have no control over components, quantities or techniques that may be applied or used. Use caution at all times. If in doubt as to your load's integrity, stop and verify it immediately!*

DISCLAIMER: *Reloading and use of reloaded ammunition can be hazardous. Read up on safety procedures and seek competent instruction. Wear safety equipment. The author assumes no liability for other persons who may use methods or information in this book.*

Printed and bound in Canada

Table of Contents

Introduction

Using once fired military brass is one way for reloaders to reduce costs. While some people will debate the merits of reloading these cases, it is one aspect of the hobby that remains popular. In the US, there are several businesses that sell military small arms ammunition or recycled components like bullets and cases. The once fired brass is picked up at the range and sold as surplus.

You can buy the brass as is or get it completely re-worked. Processed cases are cleaned, polished, resized, trimmed and the primer pockets are swaged to remove the crimp. In 2009, the full treatment was about $150 per thousand. If you plan to use military cases, this is the best way to buy them. You still need to inspect them for damage, but the rejection rate will be lower.

Some people buy unfired, Boxer primed military surplus ammunition, fire it and re-work the brass at home. The big advantage here is that the cases are fired in your rifle's chamber and not from a military gun. You get fire formed cases without the stretching. If you decide to do this, you will need to find someone that has a primer pocket swager or buy one yourself. For smaller amounts, the RCBS Primer Pocket Swager Combo costs about $25. It attaches to your reloading press and handles both large and small primer pockets. There's no need to buy a more expensive set up unless you intend to process military cases on a regular basis. For high volume users, the Dillon Super Swage 600 is a better option. It too, will swage small and large primer pockets.

Once you have the cases, perform some load work ups to determine what shoots the best from your rifle. It's important to remember that military brass has less internal volume. As a result, the load data from traditional reloading manuals should be used with care. One thing is for certain, NEVER use any maximum loads from these books using military surplus brass!

The loads in this book are **<u>NOT</u>** to be used as a substitute for a recognized reloading manual! It is imperative that you do your own tests with your own rifle. These loads are the results of numerous work ups I've performed over several years. They were re-tested and recorded so that you can see the procedures and results.

Safe Shooting!
Steve Redgwell
303british.com
2009

Cartridge Specifications

7.62x51mm

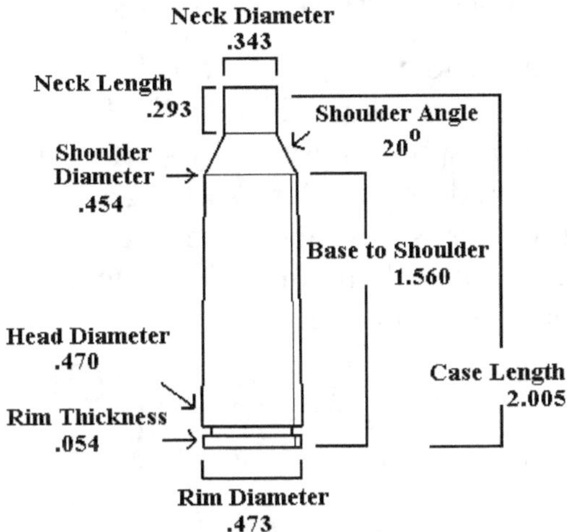

Case minimum/maximum length - 2.005 to 2.015 inches
Cartridge maximum over all length - 2.810 inches
Case capacity, in grains of water - 52.4

NOTE

Loads <u>DO NOT</u> to exceed 55,000 PSI!!

IVI cases conform to the NATO military standard, as indicated by the NATO design mark - the cross in the circle - stamped on the bottom of each.

Preparing Military Cases

7.62x51mm ammunition has been made since the 1950s. While shooting military surplus is an inexpensive way to feed your rifle, it is not accurate and the FMJ bullets are no good for hunting.

There are several factors that can affect the accuracy of surplus ammunition. The care with which individual components are made - propellant and bullets especially - affect performance in a big way. Mass produced military cartridges rarely group well. Variations in propellants or primers can affect chamber pressures and trajectories. Fluctuations in bullet weight or diameter will change downrange performance.

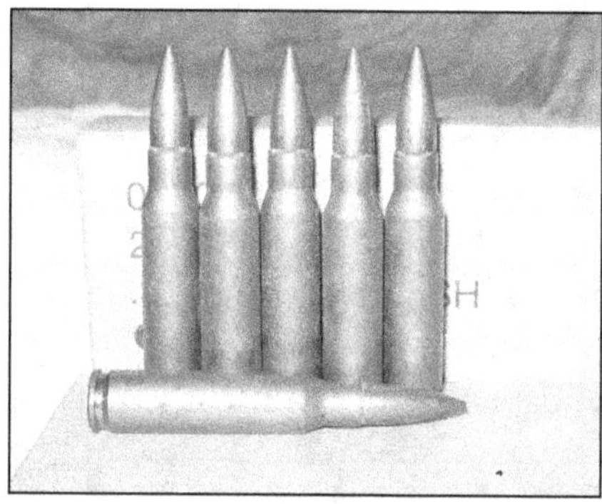

Surplus 7.62x51mm

The reason why some surplus ammunition performs so poorly is because it was improperly stored. Cartridges must be kept at a constant temperature, in a cool, dry place. They should not be subjected to swings in humidity or handled roughly. Correctly stored ammunition will always be in its original, protective packaging. That's important because it keeps out the elements.

Reloaded Ammunition

If you intend to keep reloaded ammunition for a long time, properly storing what you make is the same as for military surplus ammunition above. Find some metal ammunition boxes at your local military surplus store or buy ammo cans like those made by MTM - Case Gard. If they are in good shape, they will have a rubber seal around the inside of the lid to keep out moisture.

Your reloaded ammunition will have a very long stored life if you observe the basic, common sense steps the military or commercial factories take with their own products.

Empty Cases

Empty cases should be stored the same way to prevent corrosion. Brass should be completely prepared. They must be cleaned, the primer pocket crimps removed and the cases full length resized, in preparation for the first time they are reloaded. Remember to put a piece of paper inside the box or bag, describing exactly what was done to the cases. You cannot depend on memory - especially if a few years go by before you use them.

Preparing Fired Military Surplus Cases

Military cases need to be modified before they can be used. If your brass is unprocessed, that is, you bought it "as is", then you will have to prepare it before reloading. Preparing the brass helps to make everything the same, case to case.

Start with a visual inspection. Toss any cases that are badly damaged. Separate any headstamps that do not belong. Sometimes, commercial brass will accidentally get mixed in. Also sort any brass by year of manufacture. By the time you're done, you may have several small piles of brass that don't belong. It's best to cull them right away.

Cases have to be full length resized. Sometimes, this involves using *small base resizing dies*. These are special, full-length dies that reduce brass to its minimum contour, as designated by SAAMI (Sporting Arms & Ammunition Manufacturer's Institute). If this is not done, bulging at the case head - the result of firing cartridges in autoloading firearms - will prevent them from chambering. Standard full-length resizing dies do not always reduce case dimensions sufficiently.

There are shooters that think re-sizing military cases involves a lot of physical effort. It should not. If you have to exert a lot of force, something is not right with your set up. Either the die is incorrectly adjusted or there is insufficient case lube. Reloaders can experience pulling and tugging when the expander ball moves through the case neck. There is metal to metal contact that stresses the brass unnecessarily. The result can damage the case or distort the neck alignment, leading to excessive runout. To prevent this, lube the inside of the case necks.

Swaging the Primer Pockets

When military cartridges are loaded at the factory, their primers are swaged into place. This prevents them from backing out when used in machine guns. Before you can insert a new primer, this crimp must be removed. If you don't, the brass lip will make seating a new primer difficult or impossible. There are several tools used to realign primer pockets, but the Dillon and RCBS primer pocket swagers are the most common.

A small swaging button is pushed into the primer pocket, ironing out the brass bulge. It squares up the pocket so that new primers can be seated without hanging up. The swage or crimp is ironed out and the pocket squared.

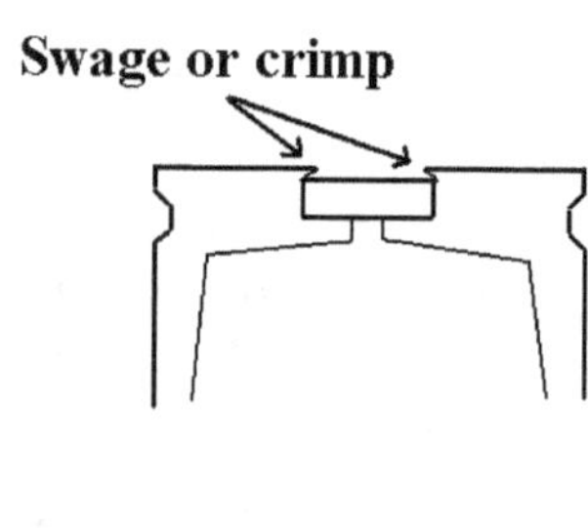

At left, the swaging button mounted on a single stage press.

Primer Pocket Uniformers

Another cutting tool used by reloaders is a *primer pocket uniformer*. When primer pockets are formed, they aren't always even or the same depth. This easy to use, handheld tool has a cutter that removes any uneven or extra brass from the bottom of the primer pocket. Performing this operation ensures that all your primer pockets are the same.

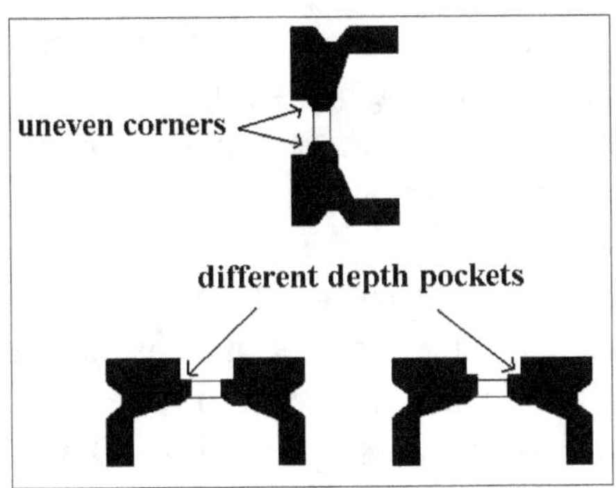

The primer pocket uniformer is inserted into the primer pocket and a few turns are all that's needed to square up the corners and/or uniform pocket's depth. There is a built in collar that assures that the blades cannot cut too deeply.

Case Trimmers

Over time, cases get longer because of repeated reloading and firing. This is a result of the thousands of pounds of pressure generated in the chamber. This pressure pushes on the case in all directions and causes the brass to stretch towards the muzzle - the path of least resistance. Responsible reloaders monitor case length as part of their overall routine.

All reloading manuals list a minimum and maximum permitted case length for safe reloading. Cases that are too long can pose a number of problems when chambering and firing. For this reason, cases must be kept trimmed for safety reasons.

Improper length can adversely affect headspace and cause dangerous pressures. The case mouth can jam at the area where the chamber and the *leade or throat* meets. This can pinch and hold the bullet, which will raise pressures. Dial or digital calipers make quick work of checking case length and are easy to use.

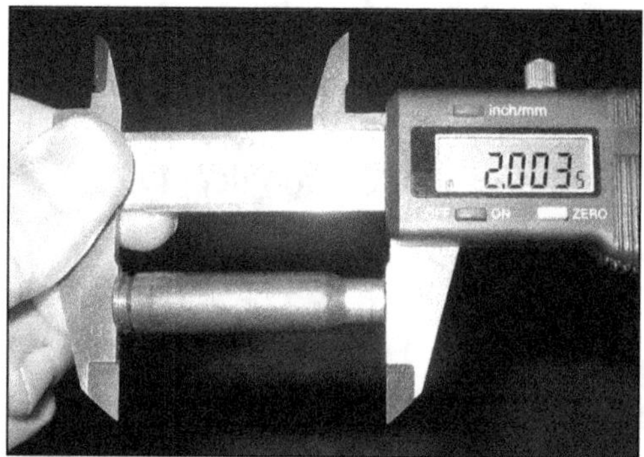

Digital calipers

Trimming can be accomplished using a number of tools made for this purpose. Case length should be checked on both newly purchased and fired, resized brass, using calipers. A good rule to follow is as follows: when 10 percent of your cases exceed the maximum length, trim back all of them to maintain uniformity.

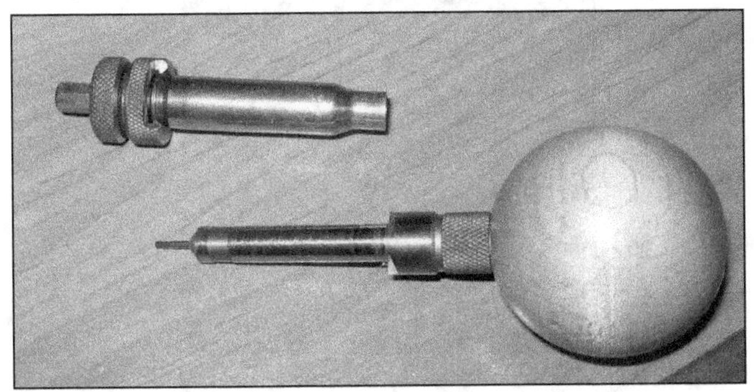

Lee Case Trimmer

There are many types of case trimmers. The Lee system is inexpensive and convenient for most trimming chores. Because military brass is thicker than its commercial counterparts, you may find it difficult to insert the trimmer pilot into the case after re-sizing. Apply gentle pressure to the pilot and twist. It will slowly work its way into the case neck.

For faster and easier cutting, trimmers can be placed in a drill chuck and turned at slow speed. You hold the blade against the case and let the drill do all the work. The wooden ball is comfortable to hold.

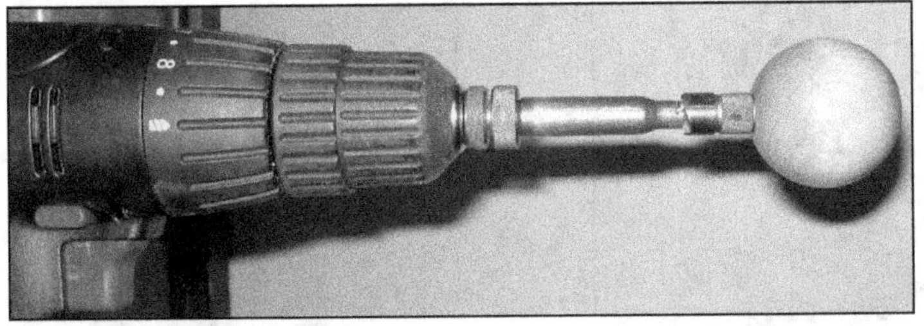

The Lee Case Trimmer attached to a cordless drill with the pilot inserted into the case.

Lee Case Trimmer Cutter blade

NOTE

Always resize cases first before trimming to length!!

Whenever you resize or trim cases to length, lightly chamfer the inside and outside of the case mouth. This removes any rough edges left by the trimming blade. A slight bevel helps the bullet enter the case when seating.

Chamfering the Case Mouth

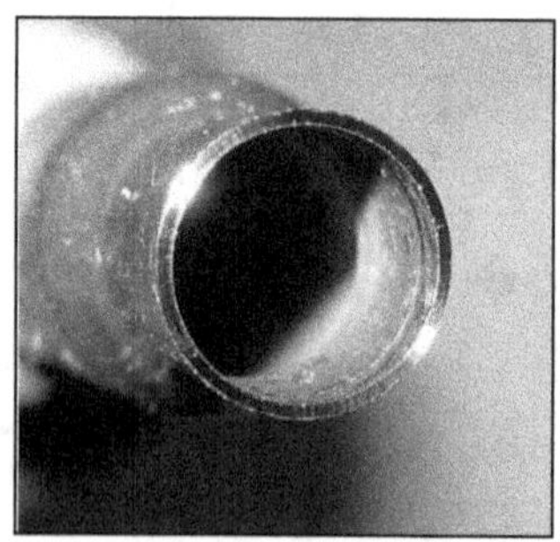 

Look closely at the case on the left and you'll see that it is trimmed to length, but not beveled.   The picture on the right shows the case mouth after being cleaned up using a chamfering tool. The inside edge has been shaped at 45 degrees to aid in bullet seating.

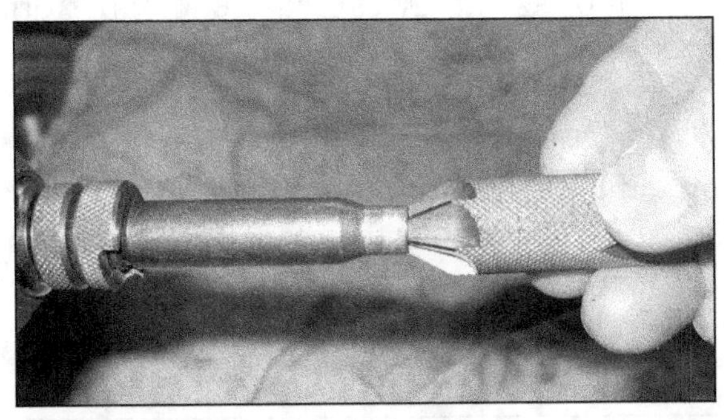

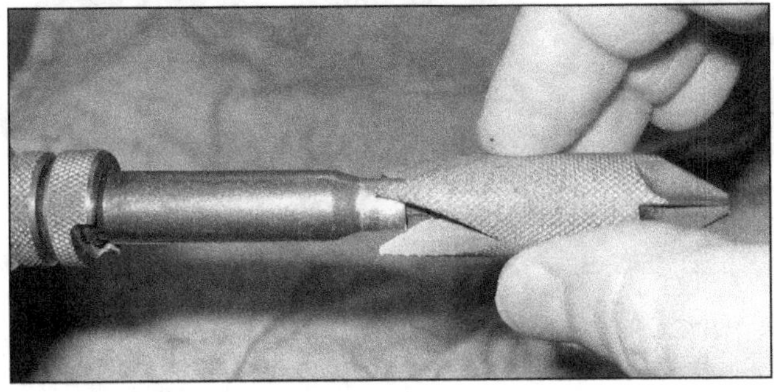

Chamfering the inside and outside of the case mouth

Flash Hole Uniformers

Military cases are mass-produced on large industrial machines. The flash holes are formed by punching a hole from the primer pocket into the interior of the case.

This leaves petals of peeled back brass inside, around the flash hole. Some shooters believe that trimming off these shards makes powder ignition more reliable, producing a more accurate cartridge.

A simple hand tool is all that's required to perform this job. Called a *flash hole uniformer*, it's a mini reamer that shears off the petals and bevels the flash hole at the web.

The trimming depth is controlled by a stop that allows the cutter to enter and cut only so far. At the other end of the tool, there is a stop collar. When it comes into contact with the web, the cutter can go no farther and the job is complete.

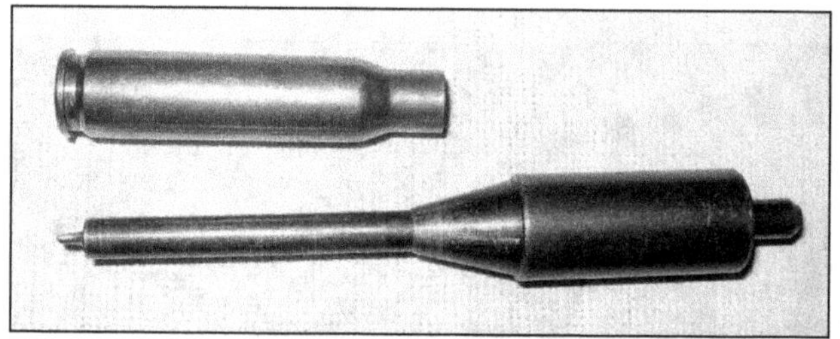

Flash Hole Uniformer

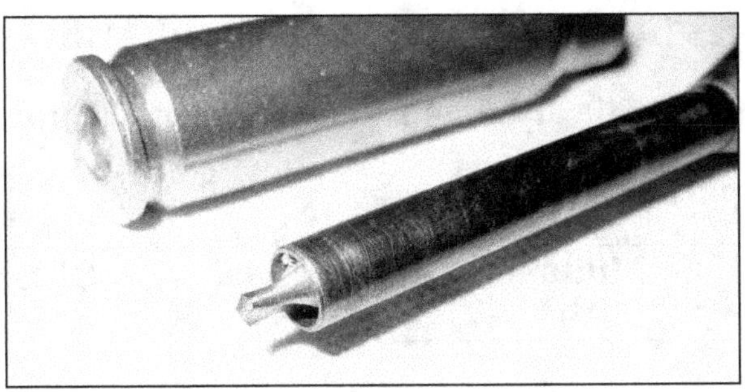

Cleaning the Cases

After the case prep is done, you can clean your cases with a case tumbler or liquid cleaning solution. It's always nice to start your work ups with uniform, shiny brass!

Differences between Commercial and Military Brass

These numbers will vary slightly between manufacturers.

Case Comparison

	Military IVI*	Commercial Lapua	Difference
Empty case wt (grains)	194.0	179.0	14.5 grains or 7.5%
Filled case wt (grains)	247.0	234.7	12.3 grains or 5%
Capacity (water wt. in grains)	53.0 fired 52.4 unfired 0.6 (1.1%)	55.7 fired 54.5 unfired 1.2 (2.2%)	2.7 grains or 5% 2.1 grains or 4%

** Industries Valcartier Industries - Canadian military brass*

Military cases have less internal capacity than their commercial cousins. We know this because they both share the same external dimensions, but the military cases weigh more. The extra weight means more brass. More brass within the same space means less internal volume.

How did I determine the numbers in the chart? Read on.

Using Water to Measure the Volume Difference

Physics tells us that the more powder you can safely burn inside a case, the faster the bullet will move. For target shooters, velocity is important as it relates to bullet drop. If you put a lot of faith in numbers, having more case volume means that sometimes, you may be able to ramp up the velocity. Sometimes, it is possible to add more powder but stay within safe SAAMI pressure limits.

For years, ammunition makers and private individuals have been using the water weight method for determining a case's internal volume. I used the same system to determine the average volume of my brass.

You may be thinking that weight and volume two different things. They are, but you can use ordinary tap water to occupy the space inside cases you wish to measure. This makes the differences easier to see. If there is a variation in volume, the amount of water added will vary. You can see this change by weighing the cases.

<u>Step One - Determine the weight of your empty fired cases</u>

Measuring ten percent of your cases will give you a good idea of the volume. If you have 100 cases, you can check 10.

Take ten fired cases - with the primers still seated - and weigh each on your scale. Record the individual weights and add up the total after you're finished. Determine the average by dividing the total by ten. This is your average empty case weight. To help, I will show you my results.

Average of my ten IVI fired cases - 194 grains

<u>Step Two - Determine the case capacity of your fired cases</u>

Take the ten cases you just weighed and fill them with water. Fill each right to the top of the neck so that the water is dished slightly inwards (concavely shaped).

Weigh the full cases. If you have a beam type scale, you can lay the case on its side if you're careful. The water won't come out.

Average of my ten water filled IVI fired cases - 247 grains

Subtract the empty case weight from the full case weight and the result will be the case capacity in grains of water.

  247 grains
<u>- 194 grains</u>

<u> 53 grains</u>   This is the average water weight of ten fired cases.

Repeat the previous steps but use commercial brass. When you compare the averages, it becomes obvious that military brass weighs more than its civilian counterpart.

From this, we can conclude two things:

1. Because commercial and military cases have the same external case dimensions, but military cases weigh more, they have more brass.

2. Because there is more brass occupying the same space, the internal volume will be less.

This is why you must never use reloading data from any book without first checking to see which type of case was used to develop the load.

Pressure Differences Caused by Changing Case Brands

What an eye opener! The powder charge, bullet and primer remained the same, but look what happened to the pressure the internal case capacity was reduced.

I took one of my most accurate loads with 155 gr. Sierra Palmas, developed using commercial Lapua cases. I changed only the case, substituting the smaller volume, IVI military brass, but adding the same amount of powder.

These volume changes show why you should always start at the minimum load listed!!

The Load
Bullet - 155 grain Sierra Palmas
Primer - Federal Match Large Rifle
Powder - 42.5 grains of H322
Cartridge over all length of 2.810 inches

Maximum Safe Pressure - 60,190 PSI

	Brand	Pressure (PSI)*	Percentage of case filled
1.	Lapua	59,710	95
2.	IVI	**65,108**	99

* computer generated pressure projection

The pressure goes from safe to over the limit! Military cases with smaller internal volumes can generate dangerous over-pressures, if using powder data from commercial reloading manuals!

This clearly demonstrates why reloaders must always start at the minimum load listed in a reloading manual and work up. Learn to recognize the pressure signs by reading instructional books, talking to experienced handloaders and studying the information pages of manufacturer's data books.

In my test, there was a change of 5938 PSI for the same powder load fired from two different cases - IVI and commercial Lapua. There was a significant change in the percentage of case filled too.

Using an equal amount of powder - 42.5 grains of H322 - it filled 95 percent of the Lapua case, but 99 percent of the IVI! When the same amount of powder is put into a smaller space, pressure will increase significantly; sometimes to dangerous levels!

Volume Differences Before and After Firing

This last part is for people that neck size their cases. If you full length resize every time, this doesn't apply to you, but makes good reading.

In the previous tests, I used fired cases. If you start with unfired or full length resized cases, how much volume difference is there?

Repeat steps one and two using unfired or full length resized cases. Compare the results to what found with the fired cases.

Here are my results:

<u>308 Winchester</u> - Commercial Case

55.7 gr - Lapua (fired)
<u>54.5 gr</u> - Lapua (unfired)
  1.2 gr difference or 2.2% more volume after firing

<u>7.62x51mm</u> - Military Case

53.0 gr - IVI (fired)
<u>52.4 gr</u> - IVI (unfired)
   .6 gr difference or 1.1% more volume after firing

Velocity can drop from the first time you use a new, unfired case to when you reload it using a neck resizing die.

SOME FINAL THOUGHTS

How much extra internal case volume is created upon firing will depend on how long your chamber measures and the thickness of the brass itself.

If you want to find out about the size of your rifle's chamber or differences between different case manufacturers, try loading 10 new cases and shoot each over a chronograph. Record every shot and average the 10. Next, reload those same cases - neck resizing only - using the same powder weight, bullet and primer and repeat the test.

For fun, find out how much powder is required to restore the original velocity. The amount of powder will increase minimally, but the powder weight will increase!

For increased precision, start your work ups with once fired cases. Fireformed cases exhibit true internal volume, align better to the bore because of their closer internal fit and are generally more accurate than full length resized or new commercial cartridges.

WARNING!

Most load data is developed using commercial cases!

Loading military brass with the same amount of powder found in reloading manuals is potentially hazardous! Dangerous overpressures may result!

WARNING!

Thinner commercial brass may rupture if shot from military rifle chambers!

Military chambers measure longer than their commercial counterparts.

Case Thickness

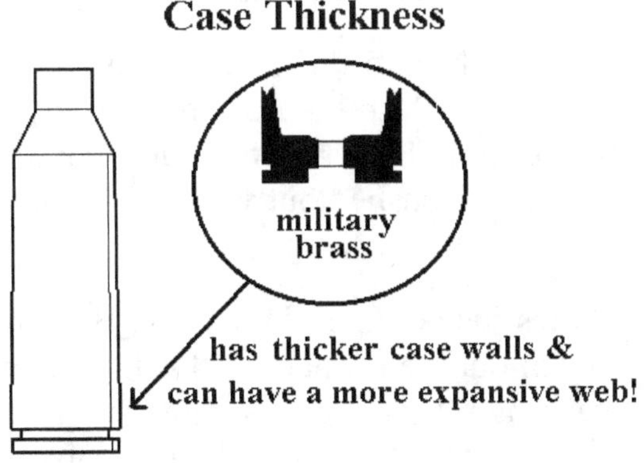

Canadian cases are made of 70/30 brass. They are 2.02 inches long and weigh approximately 224 grains.

Primers

In 1866, an American Ordnance officer, Hiram Berdan, patented the Berdan primer. Later that same year, an English Army officer, Edward Boxer, patented his priming method in the United Kingdom. Oddly, the Americans adopted the British design and the Europeans used the American one.

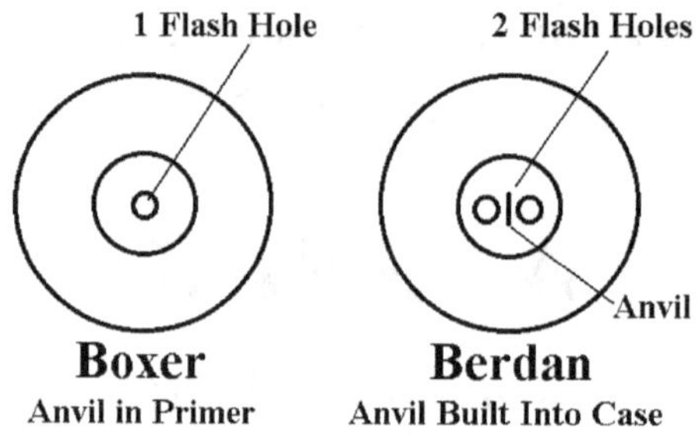

Number of flash holes – Boxer vs Berdan

If you shoot surplus 7.62x51mm ammunition to get the cases, be sure to check which kind of priming method is used. Both provide reliable functioning for military use, but which is best for reloading and how do you tell one from the other?

After firing, shine a light into the case mouth and look inside, at the bottom. Is there one flash hole or are there two? If you only see one hole, the brass is Boxer primed and good for reloading. The spent primer will be pushed out with the decapping pin when resizing.

If you see two holes inside, then the case is Berdan primed. Do not attempt to punch out the primers of this brass!! It will damage or break the decapping pin of your resizing die. The pin will push down on the solid centre of the case web and snap off.

Berdan primers are more difficult to remove - they have to be hydraulically pushed from or pried out of the primer pocket - so reloaders prefer Boxer primers.

Boxer Primers

This type is made up of a brass cup filled with primer composition. The filling is normally coated with a waterproofing compound. A tinfoil disc is placed over the primer composition and an anvil inserted part way into the cup over the foil. The anvil is friction fit into the cup to keep it in place.

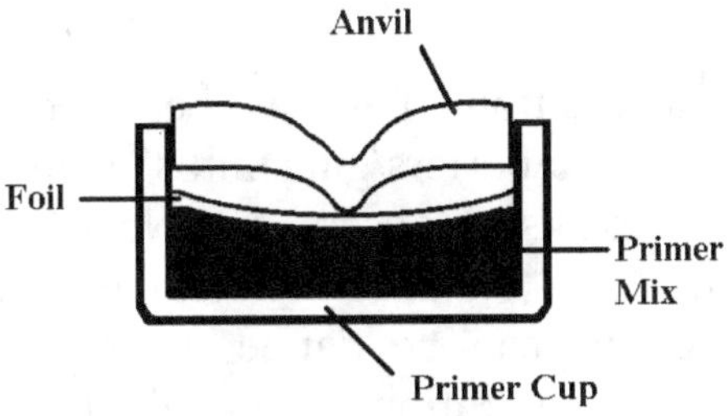

Boxer Primer

Berdan Primers

The Berdan primer is essentially the same as the Boxer, except that the anvil is formed in the primer pocket when the case is made. When the cup is inserted into the case, the anvil acts the same way when the firing pin strikes the primer cup.

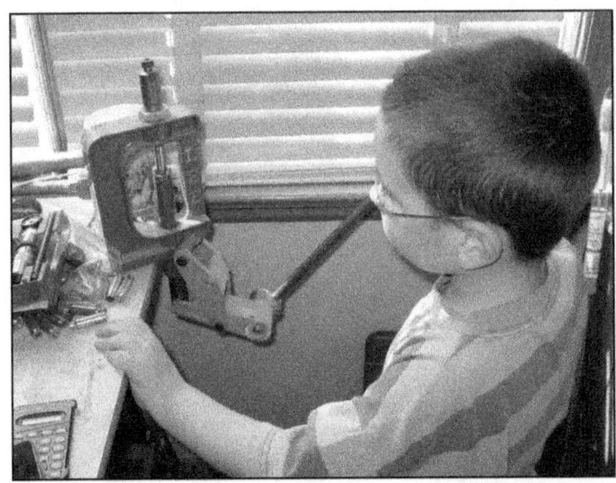

My grandson Shawn helps de-prime some cases.
He's five years old.

Important Notes about Military Surplus Rifles - Action Strengths

Military rifles chambered in 7.62x51mm vary widely in action strength.   Some were strongly built and can handle higher pressures.   Others, because of their older design, or because of rechambering, must never be loaded to levels published in most reloading manuals!

Examples of weaker actions that have been rechambered by their original owners or importers/gunsmiths include Model 93/95 Mausers (ex. FR7 Spanish Mausers) and No 1 Mk III Lee Enfields (originally 303 British - this does <u>not</u> include the Ishapore 2A/2A1 rifle).   These actions can be dangerous to fire using modern commercial factory ammunition or equivalent reloads!

The No 4 Lee Enfield was rechambered to 7.62x51mm and was proven safe to fire using military ammunition.

7.62 x 51mm Load Data

Target Loads

WARNING!!
The data presented was safe in my test rifle only!!

ALWAYS consult a recognized reloading manual
from a major component manufacturer!!

ALWAYS start at their minimum load!!
NEVER EVER start at mid range or maximum loads!!
NEVER EVER exceed their maximum load!!

Substituting <u>any</u> component for one made
by a different manufacturer can cause pressures
to change, sometimes to dangerous levels!!

Safety First!!
Be sure of what you are doing!!
If you are unsure, DON"T DO ANYTHING!!
Ask someone more knowledgeable for help!!

Load data is different for
commercial and military cases!

Loads designed for commercial cases
are dangerous when using military brass!!

Preface to the Load Data Section

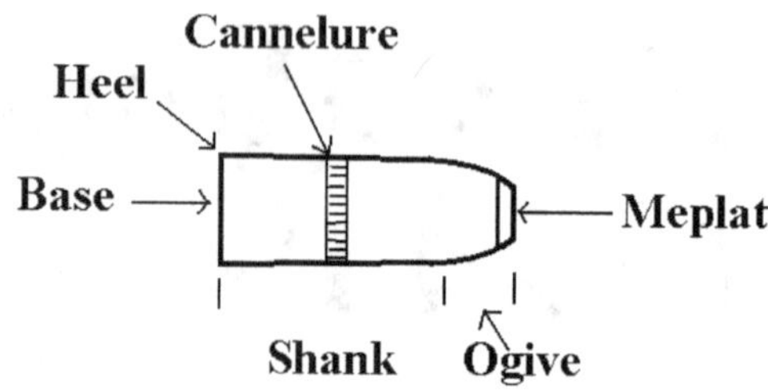

Parts of a bullet

The loads presented here are for informational purposes only. They detail load work ups using military cases that were found to be safe <u>in my rifle only</u>. Please read the *Range Notes* that precede each bullet weight. They are observations of the loads themselves and contain notes, cautions, warnings and other information.

All powders used were worked up in military cases. As noted earlier, there are significant differences between them and their commercial counterparts!

It is very important to understand that pressure can be affected by slight changes in:

Seating depth	- seating the bullet deeper into the case will increase pressure
Changing primers	- changes flame duration or intensity can make pressure go up or down
Excessive case length	- can jam the mouth of the case against the rifling, pinching the bullet and thereby increasing pressure
Bullet seated into the lands	- can cause pressure to jump radically upon ignition

These are the most common. Accidentally changing any one of these can cause pressures to change from safe to dangerous. Maximum loads fired from modern rifles with strong actions can be hazardous enough, but the same load shot from weaker military surplus rifles is asking for trouble!

WARNING!

THE LOADS WERE TESTED
USING A BOLT ACTION FIREARM
AND ARE NOT SAFE IN AN AUTOLOADING RIFLE!!

Data for .308 caliber bullets is everywhere. The purpose of this book is to detail the work I performed when developing loads for my Tikka bolt action rifle. My hope is that it will help you complete your own work ups by showing what data I recorded and retained. This is not a substitute for a recognized loading manual! If you have any questions about powder, primers or bullets when experimenting with your own loads, contact the applicable manufacturer.

The powders listed on my load charts are arranged from fastest to slowest burning.

With some loads, it is possible to safely increase the velocity by adding additional powder - typically, 0.5 to 1.0 grains. This would keep loads at, or below 60,190 PSI. With most applications, this is not necessary however.

An information table for each of the bullets I used is listed on the *Range Notes* page. It provides sectional density, ballistic coefficient and other useful facts.

All data provides velocity and energy figures. Compressed loads are indicated with an asterisk (*).

Load responsibly!
Take your time, be aware of what you're doing and have fun!

<u>Test Rifle</u>

Tikka Varmint Stainless with a 6.5-20-44 scope, Harris bi-pod.
Barrel twist - 1 in 11 inches
Barrel length - 23 ¾ inches

PRESSURE WARNING!

Bullet length has a noticeable affect on cartridge performance. These variations are the result of differences in construction or material for bullets of the same weight. Boat tailed bullets are always longer than flat based ones. Copper bullets are longer than lead. Pointed bullets are longer than round noses. Even jacket thickness changes it.

Changing a load by using same weight bullets, but made by different manufacturers, will cause velocity and pressure swings! Different brands are different lengths. As a result, when seated to the same cartridge over all length, longer bullets sit deeper in the case and take up more internal space. With shorter bullets, less space is used. In either case, chamber pressure changes. Reloaders have to watch the amount of powder they add when switching between bullets of the same weight. The deeper they sit inside the case, the higher the pressure. This can be dangerous!!

It is also important to remember that switching case brands affects pressure. Even different manufacturing runs of the same brand can cause pressure swings. Internal volume usually changes. As well, substituting primer brands will have an influence. Use caution whenever you change a component!

To summarize, whenever you change a component - brass, bullets, powders or primers - the internal pressure that develops when firing will change. If you add the same amount of powder to a case with less internal volume - either because of a longer bullet or smaller internal dimensions - pressure increases!

As a result of differences in bullet length and/or the amount of powder used, I had to alter the cartridges over all length. Bullet manufacturers always list the tested OAL in their data tables. That is why I use bullet company manuals. They are the best source of reloading information.

7.62 x 51mm Load Data

147 Grain Loads

WARNING!!
The data presented was safe in my test rifle only!!

ALWAYS consult a recognized reloading manual
from a major component manufacturer!!

ALWAYS start at their minimum load!!
NEVER EVER start at mid range or maximum loads!!
NEVER EVER exceed their maximum load!!

Substituting <u>any</u> component for one made
by a different manufacturer can cause pressures
to change, sometimes to dangerous levels!!

Safety First!!
Be sure of what you are doing!!
If you are unsure, DON"T DO ANYTHING!!
Ask someone more knowledgeable for help!!

Load data is different for
commercial and military cases!

Loads designed for commercial cases
are dangerous when using military brass!!

Range Notes

147 Grain Military FMJ BT
.308 diameter

Vital Statistics

Bullet Type	*Bullet Length*	*Sectional Density*	*Ballistic Coefficient*
Full Metal Jacket Boat Tail	1.125"	.221	.400

The data was developed to mimic M80 military ball loads.

Military (Standard Ball) Cartridge
147 grain Full Metal Jacket (FMJ)
Velocity - 2750 fps +/- 30 fps

The purpose of this section is to provide information for shooters that wish to reload pulled military bullets. If you are unfamiliar with this term, it simply means bullets that were removed from loaded military cartridges. They are sold to the public in the US by businesses like www.gibrass.com.

In Canada, a number of powders were used in 147 grain military cartridges, including WC 846. Years ago, it was said that Hodgdon bought up surplus WC 846 and marketed it as H335. I don't know if that's true. It was also said that BLC2 was newly manufactured WC 846, with excess production sold to the civilian market. H335 and BLC2 are adequate for standard ammunition, but aren't the best choice for precision cartridges.

IVI Military Cases

**PAY CLOSE ATTENTION
THAT YOU <u>DO NOT</u> USE LOADS
DEVELOPED FOR COMMERCIAL CASES
WHEN USING MILITARY BRASS!!**

WARNING!

THE LOADS WERE TESTED
USING A BOLT ACTION FIREARM
AND ARE NOT SAFE IN AN AUTOLOADING RIFLE!!

Notes about the 147 Grain Load

Military Specifications

The average grouping of 147 grain military cartridges was not to exceed 8.0 inches when shot at 600 yards. The velocity could not exceed 2750 fps, as measured at 73 feet from the muzzle.

The military bullet is 1.150 inches long and weighs 147.0 grains. The bullet is boat tailed and consists of a 90/10 lead-antimony core and gilding metal jacket. It has a milled cannelure. When assembled, the cartridge case is crimped into the cannelure.

The complete cartridge weighs 379.5 grains with an over all length of 2.800 inches.

Military Bullets Aren't the Best

Military bullets are mass produced and can vary in length and diameter. Do not expect stellar accuracy. Reloaders get these in the form of "pulled" bullets. They are physically pulled out of the case mouth using a machine. Some can be damaged.

The bullets on the left and centre are 147 gr. boat tails. The bullet on the right is a 150 flat base. All are pulled bullets that came out of the same box! The lesson? Make sure that you closely inspect <u>ALL</u> the bullets you intend to load.

Watch for sealant. It looks like black tar and should be polished off using a tumbler. Because of the generous tolerances, it's best to load these to the cannelure and crimp.

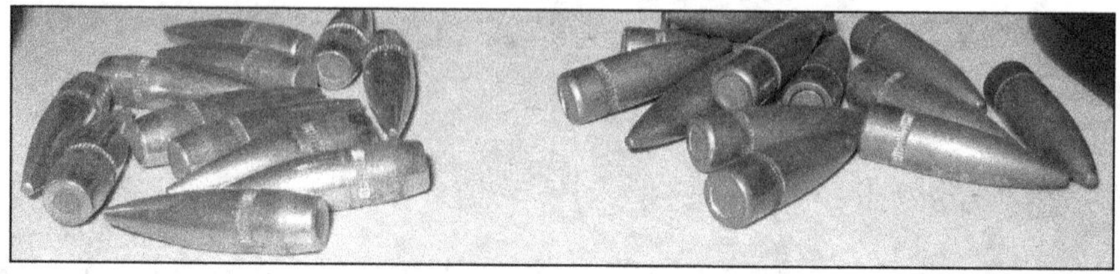

Polished bullets look nicer, but most importantly,
the sealant is gone!

Results with 147 Grain Military Loads Using Pulled Bullets

Depending on the rifle or application, they can be good for inexpensive practice or plinking. I had several hundred on my bench and decided to try some different loads using them. I also compared the performance of my reloads against the standard military load.

First, the reloaded ammunition. These are the best 100 yard groups fired from my Tikka HB target rifle. The cases were 1978 IVI (Valcartier Industries).

Group Size - Best Five Shot Group (of 200 shots tested)

1. IMR4895 - 1.06 inches
2. H4895 - 1.09 inches
3. IMR3031 - 1.11 inches
4. BLC2 - 1.14 inches
5. Re 15 - 1.15 inches
6. H322 - 1.28 inches
7. Win 748 - 1.28 inches
8. Varget - 1.44 inches
9. IMR4064 - 1.68 inches
10. H335 - 1.77 inches

Overall average for ten powders - 1.30 inches.

For comparison, I shot 50 factory military cartridges - 10 x 5 shot groups. The average velocity was 2810 fps. The average group size was 1.89 inches. The best group was 1.62 inches.

Military surplus groups

It would seem that, in my small test at least, reloading pulled military bullets improved groups. They shot better than any store bought surplus cartridges. In the past, I bought them to use for practice. You can see why I stopped. Their performance wasn't confidence building.

Dangerous Differences!!

Regardless of what you shoot, it is imperative that you work up each load! Dimensional differences between government bullets and cases, even those from the same manufacturer, can influence pressure and functionality.

The following loads were developed for my Tikka.

PRESSURE WARNING!

Bullet length has a noticeable affect on cartridge performance. These variations are the result of differences in construction or material for bullets of the same weight. Boat tailed bullets are always longer than flat based ones. Copper bullets are longer than lead. Pointed bullets are longer than round noses. Even jacket thickness changes it.

Changing a load by using same weight bullets, but made by different manufacturers, will cause velocity and pressure swings! Different brands are different lengths. As a result, when seated to the same cartridge over all length, longer bullets sit deeper in the case and take up more internal space. With shorter bullets, less space is used. In either case, chamber pressure changes. Reloaders have to watch the amount of powder they add when switching between bullets of the same weight. The deeper they sit inside the case, the higher the pressure. This can be dangerous!!

It is also important to remember that switching case brands affects pressure. Even different manufacturing runs of the same brand can cause pressure swings. Internal volume usually changes. As well, substituting primer brands will have an influence. Use caution whenever you change a component!

To summarize, whenever you change a component - brass, bullets, powders or primers - the internal pressure that develops when firing will change. If you add the same amount of powder to a case with less internal volume - either because of a longer bullet or smaller internal dimensions - pressure increases!

As a result of differences in bullet length and/or the amount of powder used, I had to alter the cartridges over all length. Bullet manufacturers always list the tested OAL in their data tables. That is why I use bullet company manuals. They are the best source of reloading information.

147 Grain Military FMJ BT
COAL - 2.800 inches
IVI Military Cases

Danger! Experimental Loads!
DO NOT USE!

Powder	Powder Weight	Grains	Velocity fps (feet per second)						
			M	100yd	200yd	300yd	400yd	500yd	600yd
IMR3031	Min	38.5	2399	2196	2002	1819	1650	1492	1352
IMR	Mid	39.5	2536	2326	2126	1936	1758	1593	1440
	Max	**40.5**	2672	2456	2250	2054	1867	1694	1533
H322	Min	37.5	2523	2314	2115	1925	1747	1582	1431
Hodgdon	Mid	38.5	2643	2428	2223	2029	1844	1672	1513
	Max	**39.5**	2762	2541	2331	2131	1941	1762	1597
Win 748	Min	41.0	2386	2184	1991	1808	1639	1483	1344
Winchester	Mid	42.0	2513	2304	2106	1916	1739	1575	1425
	Max	**43.0**	2639	2424	2220	2025	1840	1669	1510

Powder	Powder Weight	Grains	Velocity fps (feet per second)						
			M	100yd	200yd	300yd	400yd	500yd	600yd
BLC2	Min	42.0	2440	2235	2039	1854	1682	1522	1378
Hodgdon	Mid	43.0	2516	2307	2108	1919	1742	1578	1427
	Max	**44.0**	2591	2378	2176	1984	1802	1633	1477
H335	Min	40.5	2589	2377	2174	1982	1800	1632	1476
Hodgdon	Mid	41.5	2660	2444	2239	2043	1857	1685	1525
	Max	**42.5**	2730	2511	2302	2104	1914	1738	1574
H4895	Min	40.5	2528	2318	2119	1929	1751	1587	1435
Hodgdon	Mid	41.5	2628	2414	2210	2016	1831	1661	1502
	Max	**42.5**	2727	2508	2300	2101	1912	1736	1572

31

147 Grain Military FMJ BT
COAL - 2.800 inches
IVI Military Cases

Danger! Experimental Loads!
DO NOT USE!

Powder	Powder Weight Grains		Velocity fps (feet per second)						
			M	100yd	200yd	300yd	400yd	500yd	600yd
IMR4895	Min	40.5	2517	2308	2109	1920	1743	1578	1428
IMR	Mid	41.5	2601	2388	2185	1993	1810	1641	1484
	Max	**42.5**	2685	2468	2261	2065	1878	1704	1542
Varget	Min	41.0	2435	2230	2035	1850	1678	1518	1375
Hodgdon	Mid	42.0	2514	2304	2106	1916	1739	1575	1425
	Max	**43.0**	2592	2378	2176	1984	1802	1633	1477
IMR4064	Min	41.0	2486	2278	2081	1893	1718	1555	1407
IMR	Mid	42.0	2622	2408	2204	2010	1827	1657	1499
	Max	**43.0***	2758	2538	2328	2128	1938	1759	1594

*** compressed load**

Powder	Powder Weight Grains		Velocity fps (feet per second)						
			M	100yd	200yd	300yd	400yd	500yd	600yd
Re 15	Min	41.0	2495	2287	2089	1900	1725	1562	1413
Alliant	Mid	42.0	2574	2362	2161	1969	1788	1620	1465
	Max	**43.0**	2653	2437	2232	2037	1851	1679	1519

Danger! Experimental Loads!
DO NOT USE!

7.62 x 51mm Load Data

135 Grain Loads

WARNING!!
The data presented was safe in my test rifle only!!

ALWAYS consult a recognized reloading manual
from a major component manufacturer!!

ALWAYS start at their minimum load!!
NEVER EVER start at mid range or maximum loads!!
NEVER EVER exceed their maximum load!!

Substituting <u>any</u> component for one made
by a different manufacturer can cause pressures
to change, sometimes to dangerous levels!!

Safety First!!
Be sure of what you are doing!!
If you are unsure, DON"T DO ANYTHING!!
Ask someone more knowledgeable for help!!

Load data is different for
commercial and military cases!

Loads designed for commercial cases
are dangerous when using military brass!!

Range Notes

135 Grain Berger Match (308135)
.308 diameter

Vital Statistics

Bullet	*Bullet Length*	*Sectional Density*	*Ballistic Coefficient*
Match	1.082	.203	.367

IVI Military Cases

**PAY CLOSE ATTENTION
THAT YOU <u>DO NOT</u> USE LOADS
DEVELOPED FOR COMMERCIAL CASES
WHEN USING MILITARY BRASS!!**

WARNING!

**THE LOADS WERE TESTED
USING A BOLT ACTION FIREARM
AND ARE NOT SAFE IN AN AUTOLOADING RIFLE!!**

Danger! Experimental Loads!
DO NOT USE!

These light bullets were designed for smaller capacity cases, but I think that they will be good for matches shot at short range. Regardless, I provided velocity figures out to 600 yards.

I'm not really sure where this bullet will be used. It may be just the thing for recycled military cases shot from M1A/M14s or any retired 7.62x51mm surplus rifle. Recycled brass that's properly prepared should be just about perfect for military style match shooting. Maybe one or two truly serious shooters will surprise me and use Lake City or IVI cases.

These are flat base bullets.   Most competitors like to use FB bullets for short ranges - 100 to 300 yards. They were a joy to shoot after working with the mass produced 147 grain FMJBTs used in military loads. I wish that these lighter bullets were around when I was in the military and shooting competition. Recoil was soft - only 12 ft/lbs - about the same as firing a 30-30 with a 150 grain bullet.

If allowed, the Bergers would make an excellent substitute for the 150 grain bullet used in traditional loads. They are accurate, lightweight and will save your shoulder if you are shooting in an all day match. Because of their mild recoil, they would be perfect for introducing new shooters to the world of 7.62x51mm too.

When working up your loads, check with Berger and see if they have data that will work in your rifle. I like to keep my maximum loads around 55,000 PSI. www.bergerbullets.com

<h1 style="text-align:center">Group Size - Best Five Shot Group</h1>

1. IMR 3031 - 0.488 inches   6. BLC2 - 0.971 inches

2. AA2520 -   0.606 inches   7. Varget - 1.04 inches

3. Win 748 -   0.631 inches   8. H322 - 1.13 inches

4. IMR4895 - 0.689 inches   9. H4895 - 1.25 inches

5. H335 -   0.712 inches

Overall average for the nine powders - 0.835 inches

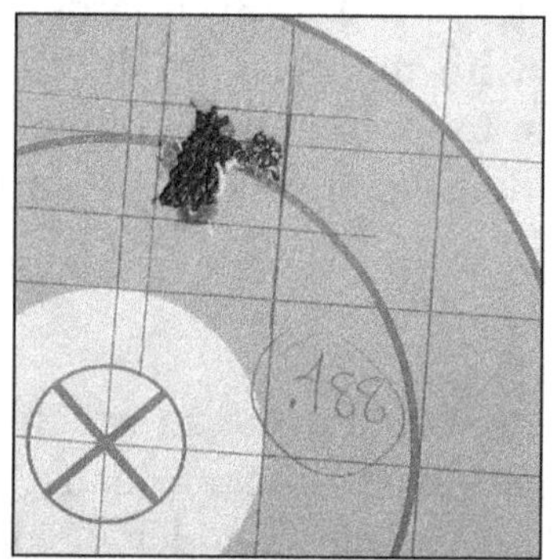

Here is the winner.

It was 42.0 grains of IMR 3031 moving at 2760 fps.

PRESSURE WARNING!

Bullet length has a noticeable affect on cartridge performance. These variations are the result of differences in construction or material for bullets of the same weight. Boat tailed bullets are always longer than flat based ones. Copper bullets are longer than lead. Pointed bullets are longer than round noses. Even jacket thickness changes it.

Changing a load by using same weight bullets, but made by different manufacturers, will cause velocity and pressure swings! Different brands are different lengths. As a result, when seated to the same cartridge over all length, longer bullets sit deeper in the case and take up more internal space. With shorter bullets, less space is used. In either case, chamber pressure changes. Reloaders have to watch the amount of powder they add when switching between bullets of the same weight. The deeper they sit inside the case, the higher the pressure. This can be dangerous!!

It is also important to remember that switching case brands affects pressure. Even different manufacturing runs of the same brand can cause pressure swings. Internal volume usually changes. As well, substituting primer brands will have an influence. Use caution whenever you change a component!

To summarize, whenever you change a component - brass, bullets, powders or primers - the internal pressure that develops when firing will change. If you add the same amount of powder to a case with less internal volume - either because of a longer bullet or smaller internal dimensions - pressure increases!

As a result of differences in bullet length and/or the amount of powder used, I had to alter the cartridges over all length. Bullet manufacturers always list the tested OAL in their data tables. That is why I use bullet company manuals. They are the best source of reloading information.

135 Grain Berger Match (308135)
COAL - 2.810 inches
IVI Military Cases

Danger! Experimental Loads!
DO NOT USE!

Powder	Powder Weight Grains		Velocity fps (feet per second)						
			M	100yd	200yd	300yd	400yd	500yd	600yd
IMR3031	Min	40.0	2544	2315	2099	1893	1703	1528	1371
IMR	Mid	41.0	2652	2418	2192	1986	1788	1606	1439
	Max	**42.0***	2760	2520	2293	2077	1873	1685	1510
H322	Min	40.0	2793	2552	2323	2106	1901	1710	1534
Hodgdon	Mid	41.0	2860	2615	2383	2163	1955	1759	1580
	Max	**42.0**	2926	2678	2442	2219	2008	1809	1625
Win 748	Min	44.0	2588	2357	2139	1931	1738	1560	1399
Winchester	Mid	45.0	2650	2416	2194	1985	1787	1605	1439
	Max	**46.0**	2712	2475	2250	2037	1836	1651	1480

*** compressed load**

Powder	Powder Weight Grains		Velocity fps (feet per second)						
			M	100yd	200yd	300yd	400yd	500yd	600yd
BLC2	Min	45.0	2671	2436	2213	2002	1803	1621	1453
Hodgdon	Mid	46.0	2712	2475	2250	2037	1836	1651	1480
	Max	**47.0**	2753	2514	2287	2072	1868	1681	1507
H335	Min	43.5	2840	2596	2365	2146	1938	1745	1566
Hodgdon	Mid	44.5	2923	2675	2440	2217	2005	1806	1623
	Max	**45.5**	3006	2763	2514	2287	2072	1869	1680
H4895	Min	42.0	2622	2390	2169	1960	1765	1585	1421
Hodgdon	Mid	43.0	2708	2471	2247	2034	1833	1648	1477
	Max	**44.0***	2793	2552	2323	2106	1901	1710	1534

*** compressed load**

38

135 Grain Berger Match (308135)
COAL - 2.810 inches
IVI Military Cases

Danger! Experimental Loads!
DO NOT USE!

Powder	Powder Weight Grains		Velocity fps (feet per second)						
			M	100yd	200yd	300yd	400yd	500yd	600yd
IMR4895	Min	42.0	2594	2363	2144	1936	1743	1565	1403
IMR	Mid	43.0	2686	2450	2227	2015	1815	1632	1462
	Max	**44.0***	2778	2538	2309	2093	1888	1699	1524
Varget	Min	42.0	2512	2285	2070	1867	1679	1505	1352
Hodgdon	Mid	43.0	2583	2353	2134	1927	1734	1557	1396
	Max	**44.0***	2653	2418	2192	1986	1788	1606	1439
AA2520	Min	43.5	2739	2501	2274	2060	1857	1670	1498
Accurate	Mid	44.5	2840	2596	2365	2146	1938	1745	1566
Arms	**Max**	**45.5**	2940	2691	2455	2231	2019	1819	1635

*** compressed load**

7.62 x 51mm
Load Data

155 Grain Loads

WARNING!!
The data presented was safe in my test rifle only!!

ALWAYS consult a recognized reloading manual
from a major component manufacturer!!

ALWAYS start at their minimum load!!
NEVER EVER start at mid range or maximum loads!!
NEVER EVER exceed their maximum load!!

Substituting <u>any</u> component for one made
by a different manufacturer can cause pressures
to change, sometimes to dangerous levels!!

Safety First!!
Be sure of what you are doing!!
If you are unsure, DON"T DO ANYTHING!!
Ask someone more knowledgeable for help!!

Load data is different for
commercial and military cases!

Loads designed for commercial cases
are dangerous when using military brass!!

Range Notes

155 Grain Hornady A-Max
155 Grain Sierra Palma (2155)

.308 diameter

Vital Statistics

Bullet	*Bullet Length*	*Sectional Density*	*Ballistic Coefficient*
A-Max	1.216"	.233	.435
Palma (2155)	1.119"	.233	.450 @ 2600 fps & above .443 from 2600 & 1800 fps
Palma (2156)	1.219"	.233	.504 @ 2700 fps & above .470 from 1800 & 2700 fps

IVI Military Cases

**PAY CLOSE ATTENTION
THAT YOU <u>DO NOT</u> USE LOADS
DEVELOPED FOR COMMERCIAL CASES
WHEN USING MILITARY BRASS!!**

WARNING!

**THE LOADS WERE TESTED
USING A BOLT ACTION FIREARM
AND ARE NOT SAFE IN AN AUTOLOADING RIFLE!!**

Danger! Experimental Loads!
DO NOT USE!

Purpose of This Test

Some police tactical teams in the US use the 155 grain A-Max, loaded in Hornady's TAP (Tactical Application Police) ammunition. I wanted to see if I could load the 155 grain bullet to the same level as the commercially produced cartridge - 2785 fps.

Presently, Sierra has two 155 grain bullets in production: The original design called the Palma - stock code 2155 - and a newer, more streamlined version, with a longer over all length - stock code 2156. According to Sierra, the older design will continue to be made, so there will be two offerings. They also said that load data is interchangeable between the two, but I would work it up separately. The newer 9 calibre ogive is 0.100 longer and will sit deeper in the case.

Group Sizes

Best Five Shot Group - Hornady 155 grain A-Max

1. H322	- 0.481 inches	6. IMR4895	- 0.762 inches
2. Win 748	- 0.514 inches	7. Re 15	- 0.774 inches
3. IMR4064	- 0.589 inches	8. BLC2	- 0.842 inches
4. Varget	- 0.606 inches	9. IMR3031	- 0.948 inches
5. H335	- 0.670 inches	10. H4895	- 0.965 inches

Overall average for the ten powders - 0.715 inches

Best Five Shot Group - Sierra 155 grain Palma (2155)

1. Win 748	- 0.459 inches	6. H4895	- 1.056 inches
2. H322	- 0.609 inches	7. IMR 4064	- 1.075 inches
3. IMR3031	- 0.845 inches	8. Varget	- 1.098 inches
4. BLC2	- 0.957 inches	9. IMR4895	- 1.347 inches
5. Re 15	- 0.987 inches	10. H335	- 1.640 inches

Overall average for the ten powders – 1.007 inches

Very interesting results. Velocities and pressures are slightly higher with the Hornady bullets. The reason is that the A-Max is longer than the Sierra and sits deeper in the case. With less internal volume, but using the same amount of powder, higher pressures are generated.

It appears that my rifle prefers the 155 grain A-Max bullets. Although the smallest test group was shot with the Sierra Palmas (0.459 inches versus 0.481 inches), the difference was only 0.022. All A-Max loads shot under an inch - an average of 0.715 inches for the ten powders - versus 1.007 inches for the Sierras. That's 29 percent smaller overall.

What does this mean? I will need to re-shoot both bullet weights again with the top three powders. I will also try the top three loads at various distances. H322 and Win 748 show the most promise - at least for short range. They were the first and second most accurate powders for both bullets.

I was successful in duplicating Hornady's TAP (Tactical Application Police) performance. Although my load chronoed 70 fps less, it was very accurate at 0.481 inches.

I will also test the new 155 grain Sierra Palma (2156) when it becomes available.

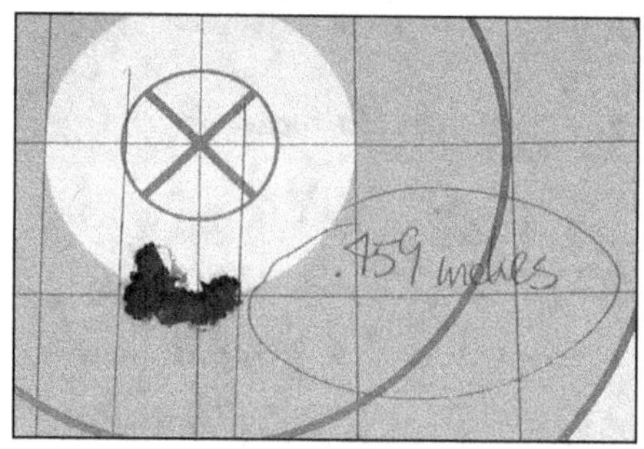

The Winner!
155 Grain Sierra Palma
0.459 inches
2582 fps
Win 748

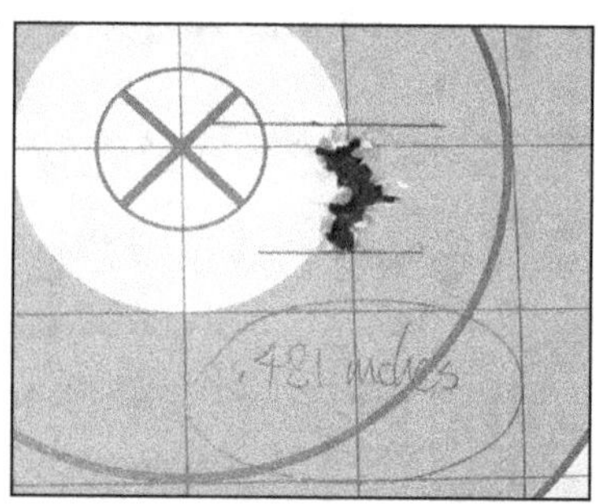

The Runner Up!
155 Grain Hornady A-Max
0.481 inches
2715 fps
H322

PRESSURE WARNING!

Bullet length has a noticeable affect on cartridge performance. These variations are the result of differences in construction or material for bullets of the same weight. Boat tailed bullets are always longer than flat based ones. Copper bullets are longer than lead. Pointed bullets are longer than round noses. Even jacket thickness changes it.

Changing a load by using same weight bullets, but made by different manufacturers, will cause velocity and pressure swings! Different brands are different lengths. As a result, when seated to the same cartridge over all length, longer bullets sit deeper in the case and take up more internal space. With shorter bullets, less space is used. In either case, chamber pressure changes. Reloaders have to watch the amount of powder they add when switching between bullets of the same weight. The deeper they sit inside the case, the higher the pressure. This can be dangerous!!

It is also important to remember that switching case brands affects pressure. Even different manufacturing runs of the same brand can cause pressure swings. Internal volume usually changes. As well, substituting primer brands will have an influence. Use caution whenever you change a component!

To summarize, whenever you change a component - brass, bullets, powders or primers - the internal pressure that develops when firing will change. If you add the same amount of powder to a case with less internal volume - either because of a longer bullet or smaller internal dimensions - pressure increases!

As a result of differences in bullet length and/or the amount of powder used, I had to alter the cartridges over all length. Bullet manufacturers always list the tested OAL in their data tables. That is why I use bullet company manuals. They are the best source of reloading information.

155 Grain Hornady A-Max
COAL - 2.810 inches
IVI Military Cases

Danger! Experimental Loads!
DO NOT USE!

Powder	Powder Weight	Grains	Velocity fps (feet per second)						
			M	100yd	200yd	300yd	400yd	500yd	600yd
IMR3031	Min	38.5	2401	2214	2035	1864	1704	1555	1418
IMR	Mid	39.5	2543	2349	2164	1988	1819	1663	1516
	Max	**40.5***	2685	2485	2294	2111	1937	1772	1619
H322	Min	37.5	2511	2319	2135	1959	1793	1639	1494
Hodgdon	Mid	38.5	2613	2416	2228	2049	1877	1717	1567
	Max	**39.5**	2715	2514	2321	2138	1962	1795	1641
Win 748	Min	41.5	2373	2187	2009	1840	1682	1534	1400
Winchester	Mid	42.5	2491	2300	2117	1942	1777	1623	1480
	Max	**43.5**	2608	2411	2224	2044	1873	1713	1563

*** compressed load**

Powder	Powder Weight	Grains	Velocity fps (feet per second)						
			M	100yd	200yd	300yd	400yd	500yd	600yd
BLC2	Min	42.5	2429	2240	2060	1888	1727	1576	1437
Hodgdon	Mid	43.5	2529	2336	2152	1975	1808	1652	1506
	Max	**44.5**	2629	2432	2243	2063	1890	1729	1578
H335	Min	41.0	2602	2406	2218	2039	1868	1708	1559
Hodgdon	Mid	42.0	2686	2486	2295	2112	1938	1773	1620
	Max	**43.0**	2769	2566	2371	2185	2007	1838	1680
H4895	Min	39.5	2439	2250	2069	1897	1735	1584	1444
Hodgdon	Mid	40.5	2517	2324	2141	1965	1798	1643	1499
	Max	**41.5**	2594	2398	2211	2032	1861	1702	1553

*** compressed load**

46

155 Grain Hornady A-Max
COAL - 2.810 inches
IVI Military Cases

Danger! Experimental Loads!
DO NOT USE!

Powder	Powder Weight	Grains	Velocity fps (feet per second)						
			M	100yd	200yd	300yd	400yd	500yd	600yd
IMR4895	Min	40.5	2469	2279	2097	1923	1759	1607	1465
IMR	Mid	41.5	2577	2382	2195	2017	1847	1689	1541
	Max	**42.5***	2685	2485	2294	2111	1937	1772	1619
Varget	Min	40.5	2390	2203	2025	1854	1696	1547	1411
Hodgdon	Mid	41.5	2476	2285	2103	1929	1765	1612	1469
	Max	**42.5***	2561	2366	2181	2003	1834	1677	1529
IMR4064	Min	40.0	2422	2234	2054	1882	1721	1571	1433
IMR	Mid	41.0	2522	2329	2145	1969	1802	1647	1502
	Max	**42.0***	2622	2425	2237	2057	1885	1724	1574

*** compressed load**

Powder	Powder Weight	Grains	Velocity fps (feet per second)						
			M	100yd	200yd	300yd	400yd	500yd	600yd
Re 15	Min	41.0	2349	2164	1988	1819	1663	1517	1384
Alliant	Mid	42.0	2430	2241	2061	1889	1728	1578	1438
	Max	**43.0***	2510	2318	2134	1959	1793	1638	1494

*** compressed load**

155 Grain Sierra Palma (2155)
COAL - 2.810 inches
IVI Military Cases

Danger! Experimental Loads!
DO NOT USE!

Powder	Powder Weight Grains		Velocity fps (feet per second)						
			M	100yd	200yd	300yd	400yd	500yd	600yd
IMR3031	Min	38.5	2351	2166	1990	1821	1657	1502	1364
IMR	Mid	39.5	2479	2288	2106	1932	1765	1603	1453
	Max	**40.5***	2606	2410	2222	2043	1871	1706	1548
H322	Min	37.5	2476	2285	2103	1929	1763	1601	1451
Hodgdon	Mid	38.5	2581	2386	2199	2021	1851	1686	1529
	Max	**39.5**	2686	2488	2297	2114	1939	1773	1611
Win 748	Min	41.5	2398	2211	2032	1861	1696	1539	1396
Winchester	Mid	42.5	2485	2294	2111	1937	1771	1608	1458
	Max	**43.5**	2572	2377	2191	2013	1843	1678	1522

*** compressed load**

Powder	Powder Weight Grains		Velocity fps (feet per second)						
			M	100yd	200yd	300yd	400yd	500yd	600yd
BLC2	Min	42.5	2403	2216	2037	1866	1701	1543	1399
Hodgdon	Mid	43.5	2515	2323	2139	1963	1797	1632	1480
	Max	**44.5**	2626	2429	2241	2061	1888	1723	1564
H335	Min	41.0	2591	2395	2208	2030	1859	1694	1537
Hodgdon	Mid	42.0	2685	2488	2297	2114	1939	1773	1611
	Max	**43.0**	2778	2577	2382	2196	2018	1848	1683
H4895	Min	39.5	2390	2203	2025	1854	1690	1533	1390
Hodgdon	Mid	40.5	2487	2296	2113	1939	1772	1610	1459
	Max	**41.5**	2584	2389	2202	2023	1853	1688	1531

155 Grain Sierra Palma (2155)
COAL - 2.810 inches
IVI Military Cases

Danger! Experimental Loads!
DO NOT USE!

Powder	Powder Weight	Grains	Velocity fps (feet per second)						
			M	100yd	200yd	300yd	400yd	500yd	600yd
IMR4895	Min	40.5	2414	2226	2047	1875	1710	1552	1407
IMR	Mid	41.5	2539	2346	2161	1984	1816	1652	1498
	Max	**42.5***	2664	2466	2276	2094	1921	1755	1593
Varget	Min	40.5	2348	2163	1987	1818	1654	1500	1362
Hodgdon	Mid	41.5	2431	2242	2062	1890	1724	1565	1419
	Max	**42.5***	2513	2321	2137	1961	1795	1631	1478
IMR4064	Min	40.0	2350	2165	1988	1819	1655	1501	1362
IMR	Mid	41.0	2461	2271	2271	1916	1750	1589	1440
	Max	**42.0***	2572	2377	2191	2013	1843	1678	1522

*** compressed load**

Powder	Powder Weight	Grains	Velocity fps (feet per second)						
			M	100yd	200yd	300yd	400yd	500yd	600yd
Re 15	Min	41.0	2327	2143	1967	1801	1636	1483	1348
Alliant	Mid	42.0	2421	2233	2053	1881	1716	1557	1412
	Max	**43.0***	2514	2322	2138	1962	1796	1631	1480

*** compressed load**

49

7.62 x 51mm
Load Data

168 Grain Loads

WARNING!!
The data presented was safe in my test rifle only!!

ALWAYS consult a recognized reloading manual
from a major component manufacturer!!

ALWAYS start at their minimum load!!
NEVER EVER start at mid range or maximum loads!!
NEVER EVER exceed their maximum load!!

Substituting <u>any</u> component for one made
by a different manufacturer can cause pressures
to change, sometimes to dangerous levels!!

Safety First!!
Be sure of what you are doing!!
If you are unsure, DON"T DO ANYTHING!!
Ask someone more knowledgeable for help!!

Load data is different for
commercial and military cases!

Loads designed for commercial cases
are dangerous when using military brass!!

Range Notes

168 Grain Hornady A-Max
168 Grain Sierra HPBT Match King
.308 diameter

Vital Statistics

Bullet Type	*Bullet Length*	*Sectional Density*	*Ballistic Coefficient*
A-Max	1.250"	.253	.475
Match King		.253	462 @ 2600 fps and above .447 between 2600 & 2100 fps .424 between 2100 & 1600 fps

IVI Military Cases

**PAY CLOSE ATTENTION
THAT YOU <u>DO NOT</u> USE LOADS
DEVELOPED FOR COMMERCIAL CASES
WHEN USING MILITARY BRASS!!**

WARNING!

**THE LOADS WERE TESTED
USING A BOLT ACTION FIREARM
AND ARE NOT SAFE IN AN AUTOLOADING RIFLE!!**

Danger! Experimental Loads!
DO NOT USE!

In the 1950s, Sierra designed a special 168 grain bullet that was to be used at international 300 meter rifle matches. It got everyone's attention in 1959 when it took first place at the Pan American Games.

In 1994, Hornady introduced the A-Max into their match line. The first was a 50 cal 750 grain bullet, and in 1995, the 7mm 162 grain A-Max. Both of these bullets had the aluminum tips which were dropped later and replaced with the current polymer tips.

I know that many competitive shooters used this bullet at one time. With more weights and manufacturers available now, it's definitely a good idea to try all the match bullets on the market.

Group Sizes

Best Five Shot Group - Hornady 168 grain A-Max

1. IMR4064	- 0.531 inches	6. Varget	- 0.812 inches
2. AA2520	- 0.567 inches	7. H4895	- 0.938 inches
3. Re 15	- 0.598 inches	8. Win 748	- 1.000 inches
4. IMR4895	- 0.625 inches	9. N140	- 1.060 inches
5. BLC2	- 0.750 inches	10. IMR3031	- 1.190 inches

Overall average for the ten powders - 0.807 inches

Best Five Shot Group - Sierra 168 grain Match King HPBT

1. AA2520	- 0.567 inches	6. IMR3031	- 0.935 inches
2. Varget	- 0.625 inches	7. IMR 4064	- 0.938 inches
3. BLC2	- 0.625 inches	8. IMR4895	- 1.070 inches
4. Re 15	- 0.875 inches	9. N140	- 1.130 inches
5. H4895	- 0.875 inches	10. Win 748	- 1.190 inches

Overall average for the ten powders - 0.883 inches

The Winner!
168 Grain Hornady A-Max
0.531 inches
2531 fps
IMR4064

The Runner Up!
168 Grain Hornady A-Max
0.567 inches
2723 fps
AA2520

The M852 military match round was designed to produce 2550 fps, +/- 30 fps, at the muzzle. Most of the loads here accomplish this easily.

Actually, there was a tie for second. Both the Hornady and Sierra bullets grouped at 0.567 inches, but the Hornady A-Max was 43 fps faster and that tipped the scales in its favour.

Just like the 155 grain bullets, my rifle preferred the A-Maxes.

If weight isn't a consideration, you would be wise to leave the 168s on your bench and stick with the lighter, 155 grain bullets.

Overall, AA2520, Reloder 15 and Varget were the most consistent. Neither bullet liked Win 748 or N140.

PRESSURE WARNING!

Bullet length has a noticeable affect on cartridge performance. These variations are the result of differences in construction or material for bullets of the same weight. Boat tailed bullets are always longer than flat based ones. Copper bullets are longer than lead. Pointed bullets are longer than round noses. Even jacket thickness changes it.

Changing a load by using same weight bullets, but made by different manufacturers, will cause velocity and pressure swings! Different brands are different lengths. As a result, when seated to the same cartridge over all length, longer bullets sit deeper in the case and take up more internal space. With shorter bullets, less space is used. In either case, chamber pressure changes. Reloaders have to watch the amount of powder they add when switching between bullets of the same weight. The deeper they sit inside the case, the higher the pressure. This can be dangerous!!

It is also important to remember that switching case brands affects pressure. Even different manufacturing runs of the same brand can cause pressure swings. Internal volume usually changes. As well, substituting primer brands will have an influence. Use caution whenever you change a component!

To summarize, whenever you change a component - brass, bullets, powders or primers - the internal pressure that develops when firing will change. If you add the same amount of powder to a case with less internal volume - either because of a longer bullet or smaller internal dimensions - pressure increases!

As a result of differences in bullet length and/or the amount of powder used, I had to alter the cartridges over all length. Bullet manufacturers always list the tested OAL in their data tables. That is why I use bullet company manuals. They are the best source of reloading information.

168 Grain Hornady A-Max
COAL - 2.810 inches
IVI Military Cases

Danger! Experimental Loads!
DO NOT USE!

Powder	Powder Weight	Grains	Velocity fps (feet per second)						
			M	100yd	200yd	300yd	400yd	500yd	600yd
IMR3031	Min	38.0	2433	2274	2122	1975	1834	1701	1576
IMR	Mid	39.0	2516	2354	2199	2049	1904	1768	1639
	Max	**40.0***	2598	2433	2275	2122	1975	1834	1702
Win 748	Min	40.0	2375	2219	2068	1923	1785	1655	1533
Winchester	Mid	41.0	2443	2284	2131	1984	1842	1709	1584
	Max	**42.0**	2510	2348	2193	2043	1899	1763	1634
BLC2	Min	41.0	2403	2246	2094	1948	1809	1678	1554
Hodgdon	Mid	42.0	2473	2313	2159	2010	1868	1733	1606
	Max	**43.0**	2542	2379	2223	2072	1927	1789	1659

* compressed load

Powder	Powder Weight	Grains	Velocity fps (feet per second)						
			M	100yd	200yd	300yd	400yd	500yd	600yd
H4895	Min	38.0	2380	2223	2073	1927	1789	1659	1536
Hodgdon	Mid	39.0	2466	2306	2152	2004	1862	1728	1601
	Max	**40.0**	2551	2388	2231	2080	1934	1796	1666
IMR4895	Min	39.5	2461	2301	2148	2000	1857	1724	1597
IMR	Mid	40.5	2539	2376	2220	2069	1924	1786	1656
	Max	**41.5***	2616	2451	2291	2138	1991	1849	1715
Varget	Min	39.0	2332	2177	2028	1885	1749	1622	1500
Hodgdon	Mid	40.0	2397	2240	2088	1943	1804	1673	1549
	Max	**41.0**	2461	2301	2148	2000	1857	1724	1597

* compressed load

168 Grain Hornady A-Max
COAL - 2.810 inches
IVI Military Cases

Danger! Experimental Loads!
DO NOT USE!

Powder	Powder Weight Grains		Velocity fps (feet per second)						
		M	100yd	200yd	300yd	400yd	500yd	600yd	
IMR4064	Min	39.0	2303	2149	2001	1859	1725	1599	1480
IMR	Mid	40.0	2417	2259	2107	1961	1820	1689	1564
	Max	**41.0***	2531	2369	2213	2062	1917	1780	1650
AA2520	Min	40.5	2552	2389	2232	2081	1935	1797	1667
Accurate	Mid	41.5	2638	2472	2312	2158	2009	1867	1732
Arms	**Max**	**42.5**	2723	2554	2391	2234	2082	1937	1798
N140	Min	39.5	2428	2270	2117	1970	1830	1697	1572
Vihtavuori	Mid	40.5*	2486	2325	2171	2022	1879	1744	1616
	Max	**41.5***	2544	2381	2225	2074	1928	1790	1660

*** compressed load**

Powder	Powder Weight Grains		Velocity fps (feet per second)						
		M	100yd	200yd	300yd	400yd	500yd	600yd	
Re 15	Min	40.0	2373	2217	2066	1921	1783	1654	1531
Alliant	Mid	41.0	2451	2292	2138	1991	1849	1716	1590
	Max	**42.0***	2529	2367	2211	2060	1915	1778	1649

*** compressed load**

57

168 Grain Sierra HPBT Match King
COAL - 2.810 inches
IVI Military Cases

Danger! Experimental Loads!
DO NOT USE!

Powder	Powder Weight	Grains	Velocity fps (feet per second)						
			M	100yd	200yd	300yd	400yd	500yd	600yd
IMR3031	Min	38.0	2383	2198	2017	1840	1676	1519	1375
IMR	Mid	39.0	2462	2274	2093	1912	1742	1584	1432
	Max	**40.0***	2541	2349	2166	1985	1810	1648	1492
Win 748	Min	40.0	2248	2068	1888	1720	1562	1412	1283
Winchester	Mid	41.0	2372	2188	2007	1830	1667	1510	1367
	Max	**42.0**	2495	2305	2124	1942	1770	1611	1457
BLC2	Min	41.0	2381	2196	2015	1839	1674	1517	1373
Hodgdon	Mid	42.0	2452	2264	2084	1903	1734	1576	1425
	Max	**43.0**	2522	2331	2148	1967	1794	1632	1477

*** compressed load**

Powder	Powder Weight	Grains	Velocity fps (feet per second)						
			M	100yd	200yd	300yd	400yd	500yd	600yd
H4895	Min	38.0	2344	2161	1980	1805	1643	1488	1348
Hodgdon	Mid	39.0	2424	2237	2057	1877	1710	1553	1404
	Max	**40.0**	2504	2314	2132	1951	1778	1618	1463
IMR4895	Min	39.5	2321	2139	1958	1785	1624	1469	1332
IMR	Mid	40.5	2449	2261	2081	1900	1731	1573	1422
	Max	**41.5***	2577	2384	2199	2018	1841	1676	1519
Varget	Min	39.0	2321	2139	1958	1785	1624	1469	1332
Hodgdon	Mid	40.0	2395	2210	2029	1851	1686	1529	1383
	Max	**41.0**	2468	2279	2099	1918	1748	1589	1436

*** compressed load**

168 Grain Sierra HPBT Match King
COAL - 2.810 inches
IVI Military Cases

Danger! Experimental Loads!
DO NOT USE!

Powder	Powder Weight Grains		Velocity fps (feet per second)						
			M	100yd	200yd	300yd	400yd	500yd	600yd
IMR4064	Min	39.0	2310	2128	1947	1775	1615	1460	1324
IMR	Mid	40.0	2407	2221	2040	1862	1696	1539	1392
	Max	**41.0***	2504	2314	2132	1951	1778	1618	1463
AA2520	Min	40.5	2483	2294	2113	1931	1760	1601	1447
Accurate	Mid	41.5	2582	2388	2203	2022	1845	1680	1523
Arms	**Max**	**42.5**	2680	2485	2295	2114	1933	1762	1603
N140	Min	39.5	2381	2196	2015	1839	1674	1517	1373
Vihtavuori	Mid	40.5*	2451	2264	2084	1903	1734	1576	1425
	Max	**41.5***	2521	2330	2148	1966	1793	1632	1476

*** compressed load**

Powder	Powder Weight Grains		Velocity fps (feet per second)						
			M	100yd	200yd	300yd	400yd	500yd	600yd
Re 15	**Min**	40.0	2341	2158	1977	1803	1641	1485	1346
Alliant	Mid	41.0	2398	2213	2032	1854	1689	1531	1385
	Max	**42.0***	2455	2267	2087	1906	1737	1578	1427

*** compressed load**

59

7.62 x 51mm Load Data

175/178 Grain Loads

WARNING!!
The data presented was safe in my test rifle only!!

**ALWAYS consult a recognized reloading manual
from a major component manufacturer!!**

**ALWAYS start at their minimum load!!
NEVER EVER start at mid range or maximum loads!!
NEVER EVER exceed their maximum load!!**

**Substituting any component for one made
by a different manufacturer can cause pressures
to change, sometimes to dangerous levels!!**

**Safety First!!
Be sure of what you are doing!!
If you are unsure, DON"T DO ANYTHING!!
Ask someone more knowledgeable for help!!**

**Load data is different for
commercial and military cases!**

**Loads designed for commercial cases
are dangerous when using military brass!!**

Range Notes

178 Grain Hornady A-Max
175 Grain Sierra Match King
.308 diameter

Vital Statistics

Bullet	*Bullet Length*	*Sectional Density*	*Ballistic Coefficient*
A-Max	1.326"	.264	.496
HPBT Match King	1.240	.270	.505 @ 2800 fps and above .496 between 2800 & 1800 fps

IVI Military Cases

M118 Match Cartridge
175.5 grain Full Metal Jacket (FMJ)
Velocity - 2550 fps +/- 30 fps

**PAY CLOSE ATTENTION
THAT YOU DO NOT USE LOADS
DEVELOPED FOR COMMERCIAL CASES
WHEN USING MILITARY BRASS!!**

WARNING!

**THE LOADS WERE TESTED
USING A BOLT ACTION FIREARM
AND ARE NOT SAFE IN AN AUTOLOADING RIFLE!!**

Danger! Experimental Loads!
DO NOT USE!

Notes about the Match Load

Military Specifications

The average grouping of M118 cartridges must not exceed 3.5 inches when shot at 600 yards. The velocity must not exceed 2550 fps, as measured at 73 feet from the muzzle. Canadian military match cartridges are loaded with either 44.0 grains of Olin WC 846 or 42.0 grains of IMR 4895.

The military bullet is 1.312 inches long and weighs 175.5 grains. The bullet is boat tailed and consists of a lead antimony core that weighs 115.5 grains and a 60 grain gilding metal jacket. It has a milled cannelure. When assembled, the cartridge case is crimped into the cannelure.

The complete cartridge weighs 390 grains with an over all length of 2.83 inches.

Cautions about Bullet Length

If you are using a computer program that asks for the bullet length as part of the computation, <u>ALWAYS</u> measure a minimum of 25 percent of the bullets in the box you are using. If you are using software that has a bullet's length pre-programmed in it, <u>DO NOT</u> trust the measurement listed! It can vary lot to lot. Like the WARNING says, longer bullets sit deeper inside the case. Pressures will be higher. This can be dangerous!!

Cautions about New or Untested Bullet Designs

If you are loading a bullet that you've never tried before, use the bullet company's data. They've tested all the powders. All bullet manufacturers can advise about the maximum loads and which propellants performed the best.

Group Sizes

Best Five Shot Group - Hornady 178 grain A-Max

1. Varget	- 0.194 inches	6. N140	- 0.655 inches
2. IMR4064	- 0.547 inches	7. H4895	- 0.664 inches
3. Win 748	- 0.601 inches	8. Re 15	- 0.674 inches
4. IMR3031	- 0.611 inches	9. IMR4895	- 0.775 inches
5. AA2520	- 0.613 inches		

Overall average for the nine powders - 0.593 inches

Best Five Shot Group - Sierra 175 grain Match King HPBT

1. Varget	- 0.360 inches	6. IMR4895	- 0.791 inches
2. Win 748	- 0.585 inches	7. AA2520	- 0.855 inches
3. N140	- 0.591 inches	8. H4895	- 1.028 inches
4. IMR 4064	- 0.693 inches	9. Re 15	- 1.058 inches
5. IMR3031	- 0.734 inches		

Overall average for the nine powders - 0.744 inches

I tried, but could not repeat the 0.194 grouping shot with the Hornady A-Maxes. The next best was 0.344 inches. Regardless, that was respectable. With either bullet, Varget was the most accurate powder in my tests.

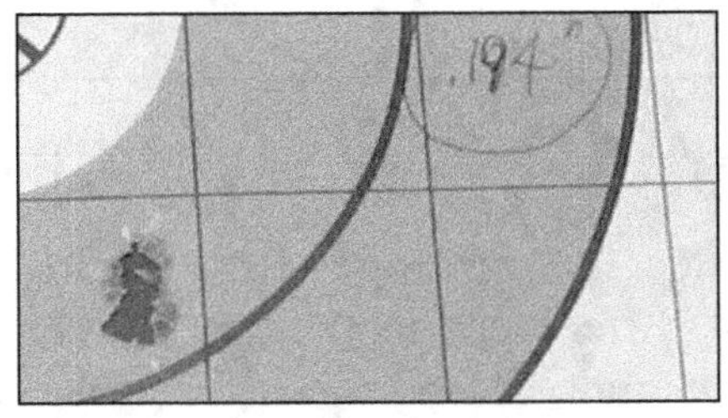

The Winner!
178 Grain Hornady AMAX
0.194 inches
2373 fps
Varget

The Runner Up!
175 Grain Sierra Match King
0.360 inches
2440 fps
Varget

Velocities were around 2400 fps. The case fill with both the loads above was 100 percent. I had thought about increasing the charge by 0.5 to 1.0 grain, but wanted to hold pressure levels to 55,000 PSI.

Often, adding 0.5 or 1.0 grain of powder will raise pressure by thousands of PSI.

NOTE

With some powders, increasing the charge would have resulted in a compressed load. I always try to be careful with compressed loads because some of the grains can be crushed when seating the bullet. This can affect how the powder burns.

As well, if there is too much powder inside, bullets will not seat correctly. Often, bullets will back out of the case, if not crimped into place. This increases the over all length of the cartridge and may cause feeding or chambering problems.

PRESSURE WARNING!

Bullet length has a noticeable affect on cartridge performance. These variations are the result of differences in construction or material for bullets of the same weight. Boat tailed bullets are always longer than flat based ones. Copper bullets are longer than lead. Pointed bullets are longer than round noses. Even jacket thickness changes it.

Changing a load by using same weight bullets, but made by different manufacturers, will cause velocity and pressure swings! Different brands are different lengths. As a result, when seated to the same cartridge over all length, longer bullets sit deeper in the case and take up more internal space. With shorter bullets, less space is used. In either case, chamber pressure changes. Reloaders have to watch the amount of powder they add when switching between bullets of the same weight. The deeper they sit inside the case, the higher the pressure. This can be dangerous!!

It is also important to remember that switching case brands affects pressure. Even different manufacturing runs of the same brand can cause pressure swings. Internal volume usually changes. As well, substituting primer brands will have an influence. Use caution whenever you change a component!

To summarize, whenever you change a component - brass, bullets, powders or primers - the internal pressure that develops when firing will change. If you add the same amount of powder to a case with less internal volume - either because of a longer bullet or smaller internal dimensions - pressure increases!

As a result of differences in bullet length and/or the amount of powder used, I had to alter the cartridges over all length. Bullet manufacturers always list the tested OAL in their data tables. That is why I use bullet company manuals. They are the best source of reloading information.

178 Grain Hornady A-Max
COAL - 2.810 inches
IVI Military Cases

Danger! Experimental Loads!
DO NOT USE!

Powder	Powder Weight	Grains	Velocity fps (feet per second)						
			M	100yd	200yd	300yd	400yd	500yd	600yd
IMR3031	Min	36.0	2275	2142	2012	1887	1769	1656	1549
IMR	Mid	37.0	2369	2233	2101	1973	1849	1733	1622
	Max	**38.0***	2463	2323	2188	2058	1931	1810	1695
Win 748	Min	38.0	2164	2034	1908	1789	1675	1567	1464
Winchester	Mid	39.0	2257	2124	1996	1871	1753	1642	1535
	Max	**40.0**	2350	2214	2083	1955	1833	1717	1607
H4895	Min	36.0	2264	2131	2002	1878	1759	1647	1540
Hodgdon	Mid	37.0	2328	2193	2062	1935	1814	1699	1590
	Max	**38.0**	2392	2255	2122	1994	1869	1752	1640

*** compressed load**

Powder	Powder Weight	Grains	Velocity fps (feet per second)						
			M	100yd	200yd	300yd	400yd	500yd	600yd
IMR4895	Min	37.5	2304	2170	2040	1914	1794	1680	1571
IMR	Mid	38.5	2389	2252	2119	1991	1867	1749	1637
	Max	**39.5**	2474	2334	2199	2068	1941	1819	1704
Varget	Min	37.5	2251	2118	1990	1866	1748	1637	1530
Hodgdon	Mid	38.5	2312	2177	2047	1921	1800	1686	1577
	Max	**39.5**	2373	2236	2104	1976	1853	1736	1625
IMR4064	Min	37.5	2263	2131	2002	1878	1759	1647	1540
IMR	Mid	38.5	2356	2220	2088	1961	1838	1722	1612
	Max	**39.5***	2449	2310	2175	2045	1919	1798	1684

*** compressed load**

178 Grain Hornady A-Max
COAL - 2.810 inches
IVI Military Cases

Danger! Experimental Loads!
DO NOT USE!

Powder	Powder Weight Grains		Velocity fps (feet per second)						
			M	100yd	200yd	300yd	400yd	500yd	600yd
N140	Min	37.5	2260	2127	1999	1874	1756	1644	1537
Vihtavuori	Mid	38.5	2339	2204	2072	1945	1824	1708	1598
	Max	**39.5***	2418	2280	2146	2017	1892	1773	1660
AA2520	Min	38.5	2379	2242	2110	1982	1858	1741	1630
Accurate	Mid	39.5	2434	2295	2161	2031	1906	1786	1673
Arms	**Max**	**40.5**	2489	2348	2213	2081	1954	1832	1716
Re 15	Min	38.0	2228	2096	1969	1845	1729	1618	1512
Alliant	Mid	39.0	2303	2170	2040	1914	1794	1680	1571
	Max	**40.0***	2377	2240	2108	1980	1856	1739	1628

*** compressed load**

175 Grain Sierra Match King
COAL - 2.810 inches
IVI Military Cases

Danger! Experimental Loads!
DO NOT USE!

Powder	Powder Weight Grains		Velocity fps (feet per second)						
			M	100yd	200yd	300yd	400yd	500yd	600yd
IMR3031	Min	37.5	2378	2210	2050	1896	1750	1611	1481
IMR	Mid	38.5	2470	2299	2136	1979	1828	1685	1550
	Max	**39.5**	2561	2387	2220	2059	1905	1758	1619
Win 748	Min	39.5	2311	2147	1990	1838	1695	1559	1433
Winchester	Mid	40.5	2378	2210	2050	1896	1750	1611	1481
	Max	**41.5**	2445	2275	2113	1956	1807	1665	1531
H4895	Min	37.5	2350	2184	2025	1872	1728	1590	1461
Hodgdon	Mid	38.5	2396	2229	2068	1913	1766	1626	1495
	Max	**39.5**	2442	2273	2110	1954	1805	1663	1529

* compressed load

Powder	Powder Weight Grains		Velocity fps (feet per second)						
			M	100yd	200yd	300yd	400yd	500yd	600yd
IMR4895	Min	39.0	2403	2235	2074	1919	1772	1632	1500
IMR	Mid	40.0	2475	2304	2140	1983	1832	1689	1554
	Max	**41.0**	2547	2373	2207	2047	1893	1747	1608
Varget	Min	39.0	2328	2163	2005	1853	1709	1573	1445
Hodgdon	Mid	40.0	2384	2217	2057	1902	1756	1617	1486
	Max	**41.0**	2440	2273	2110	1954	1805	1663	1529
IMR4064	Min	39.5	2404	2235	2074	1919	1772	1632	1500
IMR	Mid	40.5	2485	2314	2150	1992	1841	1697	1561
	Max	**41.5***	2565	2391	2223	2063	1908	1762	1622

* compressed load

<h1 style="text-align:center">175 Grain Sierra Match King</h1>

COAL - 2.810 inches
IVI Military Cases

<h1 style="text-align:center">Danger! Experimental Loads!
DO NOT USE!</h1>

Powder	Powder Weight Grains		Velocity fps (feet per second)						
			M	100yd	200yd	300yd	400yd	500yd	600yd
N140	Min	39.5	2388	2221	2060	1906	1759	1620	1489
Vihtavuori	Mid	40.5	2451	2281	2118	1962	1812	1670	1536
	Max	**41.5***	2514	2342	2176	2017	1865	1721	1583
AA2520	Min	40.0	2432	2263	2101	1945	1797	1655	1521
Accurate	Mid	41.0	2497	2326	2161	2002	1851	1707	1570
Arms	**Max**	**42.0**	2562	2387	2220	2059	1905	1758	1619
Re 15	Min	39.5	2311	2147	1990	1838	1695	1559	1433
Alliant	Mid	40.5	2396	2229	2068	1913	1766	1626	1495
	Max	**41.5***	2481	2310	2146	1989	1837	1694	1558

* compressed load

Quick Reference Definitions

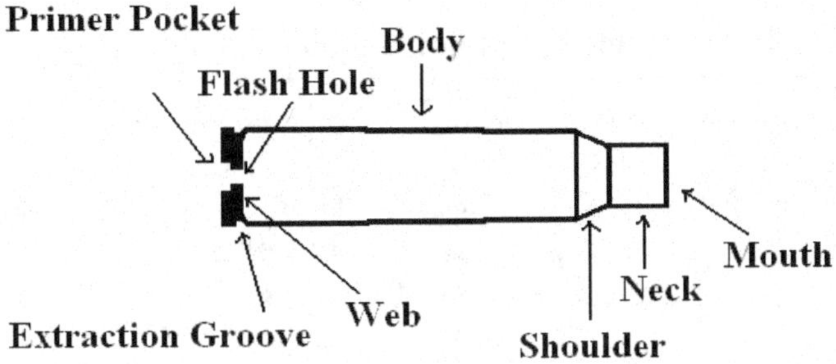

Parts of a case

Annealing - After repeated use and resizing, brass can become brittle. Annealing is the heating of the case neck after work hardening to restore its suppleness.

Ball - A military term for full metal jacketed ammunition. It is derived from the days when rounded shot was fired from black powder firearms.

Ball Powder - This is a copyrighted name describing double base spherical or flattened spherical powder from Olin Corporation.

Ballistics - The study of projectiles in motion. There are three areas.

Interior Ballistics - the study of effects from primer ignition to bullet exit from the barrel.
Exterior Ballistics - the study of bullet movement from the bullet's exit from barrel to the target.
Terminal Ballistics - the study of bullet impact on the target.

Ballistic Coefficient - This is a mathematical number that represents a projectile's ability to overcome air resistance. The higher the number, the more streamlined flight. This translates into higher retained energy at impact.

Bearing Surface - The area of the bullet in contact with the bore when moving through the barrel. A larger bearing surface more easily stabilizes a bullet along its longitudinal axis.

Base - The flat, bottom section of a bullet that sits inside the case.

Bell - Expanding the case mouth to aid in bullet seating.

Bevelling – Angling the squared, inside edge of a case mouth after trimming to length, to aid in bullet seating. Usually 45 degrees. Also referred to as chamfering.

Bolt Thrust - The rearward force applied to the bolt face as the powder burns in a case.

Bore - The inside of a barrel. In rifled barrels, the diameter before the rifling is cut.

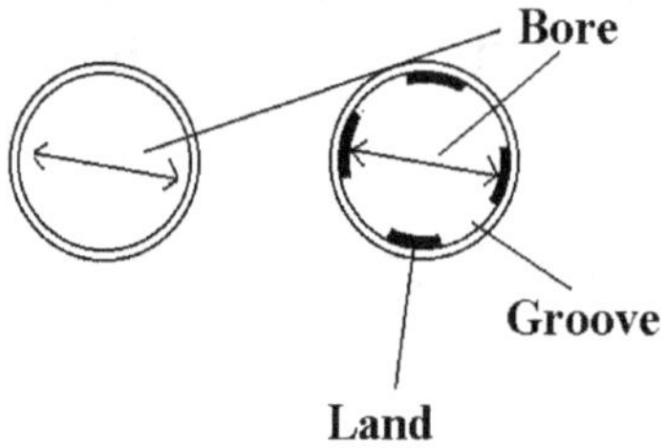

Bullet Pull - The force needed to release a bullet from the mouth of a loaded cartridge.

Burn Rate - The rate at which a powder burns compared to other powders – also known as Relative Quickness. eg. in the burn rate chart, Win 231 has a faster burn rate than Win 760.

Calibre or Caliber - The diameter of a bullet or the diameter of gun's bore. It can be expressed in inches or millimeters.

Cannelure - The grooved, circumferential portion of the bullet located on the shank. Used as a crimping mark or for lubrication.

Case Forming - Changing the shape and dimensions of an existing case to create a new case for a different cartridge.

Chamber Casting - The hardened result of material poured into a firearm's chamber. The casting is used to check chamber's condition or dimensions.

Chamfer - Bevelling or shaping of the inside of a case mouth to aid in bullet seating.

Choke - The muzzle constriction of a shotgun barrel, designed to control the spread of the shot charge.

Chronograph - An electronic device used to determine the velocity of a projectile in flight.

Compressed Charge - A powder charge that is packed into the case when seating the bullet. A compressed load exceeds 100 % load density.

Deflection - The influence of wind on bullet flight after it has left the barrel.

Drift - The influence of bullet rotation or "spin" that moves a bullet off of its original line of departure from the barrel.

Duplex Load - Using two different burning powders in the same case when loading. This is dangerous and often results in unpredictable, widely varying pressures. Not a good practice!

Energy - An expression of the amount of work that can be done by a bullet for a given velocity and bullet weight.

$$\text{Kinetic (Impact) Energy (in foot/pounds)} = \frac{\text{Velocity}^2 \times \text{Bullet Weight (in grains)}}{450400}$$

Fireforming - Shaping cases to provide a custom fit within a chamber.

Freebore - The distance that a bullet travels when fired, from its seated position within the case mouth to where it contacts the barrel rifling.

Groove - Cuts in the barrels bore which induce spin as the bullet travels through it.

Hangfire - A delay in cartridge ignition after the primer has been struck by the firing pin.

Heel - The area of a bullet where the base meets the shank.

Improved Cartridge - A cartridge case that has been altered from the original. It normally involves reducing the body taper, increasing the shoulder angle, or both. This results in increased powder capacity and velocity with no significant change in internal pressure.

IMR - Improved Military Rifle. A cylindrical, stick powder.

Lands - The portion of the bore that remains after the grooves have been cut.

Leade - See Throat.

Mean Radius - The average radius of a group of shots measured from the centre of the group.

Meplat - The diameter of the pointed end of a bullet. It can be negligible in a spitzer type, or large as in a flat nosed bullet.

Minute of Angle - Unit of measurement equal to 1/60th of a degree. At 100 yards it would be 1.047 inches but is expressed as 1 inch by most shooters.

Mushroom - The expansion of a bullet at and after impact.

Muzzle Blast - The blast of hot gases, noise and flame at the muzzle of a firearm after discharge.

Muzzle Energy - An expression of the amount of work that can be done by the bullet at the muzzle. Measured in foot-pounds.

Ogive - The curved area from the straight section (shank) of a bullet to its meplat.

Oil (Lube) Denting - Denting caused by excessive case lubricant during the resizing operation.

Primer Leak - Pressure (gas) venting from around the primer. It can be a result of excessively high pressures, oversize primer pockets or undersize primers.

Proof Cartridge - A specially loaded cartridge, used to test new or refurbished firearms. Usually loaded to pressures 25% above maximum.

Rifling - The spiral cuts found in the barrels of most firearms to impart bullet spin.

Round - A military term for cartridge.

Runout - When the bullet is not in line with the center axis of the bore. This can be caused by an off centre case neck or improper alignment when seating the bullet.

Rupture - A failure or break in a case wall

SAAMI - Sporting Arms & Ammunition Manufacturer's Institute

Sabot - A carrier used for bullets smaller than the barrel's calibre so that they may be shot from that barrel.

Seating Depth - The depth to which a bullet is seated in a case at loading.

Sectional Density - The bullet's weight (in pounds) divided by the square of its diameter (in inches). In general terms, the higher the sectional density, the better the penetration.

$$\text{Sectional Density} = \frac{\text{Bullet Weight}}{\text{Bullet Diameter}^2} \quad \begin{array}{l} \text{(in pounds)} \\ \text{(in inches)} \end{array}$$

Shank - The straight, cylindrical section of the bullet running from the heel to the ogive.

Shock - The effect of transferring a bullet's energy to its target.

Throat - The area of the bore directly in front of the chamber but before the rifling. This area can vary in size between firearms of the same calibre.

Wildcat - A cartridge whose case is altered in such a way that it is not available from commercial suppliers.

Work Hardening - The result of repeated working of the brass in firing and resizing. This causes the brass to become brittle and can cause cracking and breaking.

Work Ups - The process of load development - devising and building low pressure loads and increasing them slowly to determine the safe maximum level.

Powder Burn Rates

1. Norma R1
2. Winchester WAALite
3. Vihtavuori N310
4. Alliant e3
5. Hodgdon TITEWAD
6. Alliant Red Dot
7. Hodgdon CLAYS
8. Hi-Skor 700-X
9. Alliant Bullseye
10. Hodgdon TITEGROUP
11. Alliant American Select
12. AA Solo 1000
13. Alliant Green Dot
14. IMR, Co Trial Boss
15. Win Super Handicap
16. Hodgdon INTERNATIONAL
17. PB
18. Vihtavuori N320
19. Winchester WST
20. AA No. 2
21. SR 7625
22. Hodgdon HP-38
23. Winchester 231
24. Alliant 20/28
25. Alliant Unique
26. Hodgdon UNIVERSAL
27. Alliant Power Pistol
28. Vihtavuori N330
29. Alliant Herco
30. Winchester WSF
31. Vihtavuori N340
32. Hi-Skor 800-X
33. SR4756
34. AA No. 5
35. Hodgdon HS-6
36. Vihtavuori 3N37
37. Vihtavuori N350
38. Hodgdon HS-7
39. Vihtavuori 3N38
40. Alliant Blue Dot
41. AA No. 7
42. Hodgdon LONGSHOT
43. Alliant 410
44. Alliant 2400
45. AA No. 9
46. NORMA R123
47. Vihtavuori N110
48. Hodgdon LIL'GUN
49. Hodgdon H110
50. Winchester 296
51. IMR 4227
52. Hodgdon H4227
53. SR4759
54. AA 1680
55. NORMA 200
56. Alliant Reloder 7
57. IMR4198
58. Hodgdon H4198
59. Vihtavuori N120
60. Hodgdon H322
61. AA 2015BR
62. Vihtavuori N130
63. IMR3031
64. Vihtavuori N133
65. Hodgdon BENCHMARK
66. Hodgdon H335
67. AA 2230
68. AA 2460
69. Hodgdon H4895
70. Vihtavuori N530
71. IMR4895
72. Vihtavuori N135
73. Alliant Reloder 12
74. IMR4320
75. AA 2495BR
76. IMR4064
77. NORMA 202
78. AA 2520
79. Alliant Reloder 15
80. Vihtavuori N140
81. Hodgdon VARGET
82. Winchester 748
83. Hodgdon BL-C(2)
84. Hodgdon H380
85. IMR4007SSC
86. Vihtavuori N540
87. Winchester 760
88. Hodgdon H414
89. Vihtavuori N150
90. AA 2700
91. IMR4350
92. Hodgdon H4350
93. AA 4350
94. NORMA 204
95. Hodgdon HYBRID 100V
96. Vihtavuori N550
97. Alliant Reloder 19
98. IMR4831
99. AA 3100
100. Vihtavuori N160
101. Hodgdon H4831 & H4831SC
102. Win Supreme 780
103. NORMA MRP
104. Alliant Reloder 22
105. Vihtavuori N560
106. Vihtavuori N165
107. IMR7828
108. Vihtavuori N170
109. Hodgdon H1000
110. Hodgdon RETUMBO
111. Vihtavuori N570
112. AA 8700
113. Hodgdon H870
114. Vihtavuori 24N41
115. Hodgdon H50BMG
116. Hodgdon US869
117. Vihtavuori 20N29

Saskatchewan Dynamite

I needed some dynamite to take out several tree stumps last fall. I had to be finished blastin' before the weather turned too cold and huntin' season started. I figured on using regular sticks, but my buddy Riley said no, that they got special plastic stumpin' bags at the hardware store now.

"Old Alfred Nobel would be proud of you, Steve! Them bags are the ones with granulated dynamite kibbles inside. Just like on the TV!" he said. "You could make a slurry. Got any diesel?" he asked. I farm four sections! Of course I got diesel, and nodded my head. "Well, heck, don't stand there lookin' dumber than you are. Let's go!"

So Riley and me jumped in my pick up and drove to the Home Hardware. When we arrived, I seen that Old Norm was workin'. Well, if you call sittin' on a lawn chair talkin' to garden gnomes workin'. He's older than dirt, and frankly, not all there...if you catch my meanin'. But since Monday was the owner's weekly bowlin' luncheon and tournament afternoon, who else would be watchin' the place?

"Hi Norm!" I said. "Sure is cold out today. Cold enough to freeze the brass off a bald monkey!"

He just ignored me and kept fightin' with a small box, talkin' to himself. "They snapped right off! Damn French made crap!" Norm must have finally noticed that we was standin' beside him 'cause he looked at Riley and said, "You know, there was a time when imported stuff was really high quality and fancy. Look at this!"

The three of us stood there starin' into a box full of aluminium nails. Now, I'm not talkin' about nails that you use to nail aluminium with. I'm talkin' about nails MADE of aluminium. French made aluminium nails. What the heck would they be for?

"Norm," I said, "I'd like to help you with them things, but I'm in a rush. You got any dynamite in the back? See, I gotta..."

"No, no, don't tell me! You're goin' to blow up manure piles again, ain't ya? Ha ha! I'll never forget when you graduated from high school. While all your friends was at the dance, you and that stupid kid...um...what was his name? Oh yeah, Spoorface Jones, the two of you come in for to buy some dynamite that day too. He had a face that could curdle milk!" Then he spun around and looked right at my buddy Riley. "You never met him. You're from Moose Jaw, ain't ya?"

He continued tellin' his story, starin' intently at my very confused friend. "Spoorface was the youngest boy of a government fellow what tried to grow pineapples around here. Hah! A pineapple farm in Saskatchewan! And they called me an id-yut!"

As he finished speakin', a bit of drool ran out the corner of his mouth. Then he started laughin', but stopped almost immediately.

"What ever happened to him, Steve?"

"I don't know, Norm."

"Don't matter. Dumber than a bag of hammer handles he was. His family moved here all the way from Ottawa. Spoorface's daddy was a know-it-all government man, come to start a job program. Damn Liberals! What id-yut would plant pineapples here? Fish farmin' maybe. Heck, it worked in British Columbia!"

I was puzzled and said, "Come on Norm, BC's on the coast."

"The coast of what?"

"The coast! The west coast. The Pacific coast! You know, the coast of BC - where they have all that water..."

"Oh yeah, that coast. That's where them damn hippies live! I bin tellin' you boys since you was kids not to trust no one from a place with all that water. It ain't healthy. See, if I was the Prime Minister, I'd be sellin' that water to the States..."

"But Norm, it's salt water."

"So? At least they wouldn't have to drill down hundreds of feet and pump it out. Why, when I was your age, our fathers would make us dig a hole so deep it took you the better part of a week to get out! They lowered us down on a big rope and made us fill water buckets by hand..."

And that's how it went for the rest of the day. We spent the whole afternoon listenin' to old Norm. Riley said that he was the reason why Manitoba and Saskatchewan never became big industrial superpowers inside of the Dominion of Canada. Too many kooks like Norm around, he said.

Well sir, days like that made me wonder how humans managed to survive this long. Okay, if my mother was still alive, she'd likely have washed my mouth out with soap by now, for thinkin' something unkind like that about my elders. Oh heck, Norm's a good guy and all. He's just what my uncle used to call 'touched by the angels'. You know, the porch light's on but nobody's home...Sorry mom.

And you know what? After all was said and done, I still never got no dynamite…

Bibliography

Alliant Powder Company (1996), *Reloader's Guide*, Alliant Techsystems, Radford, Virginia, USA

Barnes, Frank, C. (1997), *Cartridges of the World - 8th Edition*, DBI Books, Northbrook, Illinois, USA, ISBN 0-87349-178-5

Blount Inc. Sporting Equipment Division, (1995), *Speer Rifle and Pistol Reloading Manual - Number 12*, Lewiston, Idaho, USA

Donnelly, John, J (1987), The Handloader's Manual of Cartridge Conversions, Stoeger Publishing, Wayne, New Jersey, USA

Hodgdon Powder Company (1992), Hodgdon *Data Manual - 26th Edition*, Shawnee Mission, Kansas, USA

Hornady Manufacturing Company (1996), *Hornady Handbook of Cartridge Reloading 4th Edition*, Grand Island, Nebraska, USA

Redgwell, Stephen E. (2002) 303 British & 7.62/308 Winchester Cases. http://www.303british.com/id39.html (29 Dec 2007)

Sierra Bullet Company (2003), *Sierra Rifle Reloading Manual - 5th Edition*, Sedalia, Missouri, USA

Wikipedia. (2008) Internal Ballistics.
http://en.wikipedia.org/wiki/Internal_ballistics, (23 Jan, 2008)

www.ingramcontent.com/pod-product-compliance
Lightning Source LLC
Chambersburg PA
CBHW061724250726

48657CB00002B/765